Jim Shirley

Those Were the Days

ALSO BY JILL SHEELEY

Christmas in Aspen

Tastes of Aspen

Lighter Tastes of Aspen

Adventures of Fraser the Yellow Dog:
Rescue on Snowmass Mountain

Adventures of Fraser the Yellow Dog:
Rescue on Vail Mountain

Adventures of Fraser the Yellow Dog:
Rescue on Star Mountain

Adventures of Fraser the Yellow Dog:
Rescue on Aspen Mountain

Adventures of Fraser the Yellow Dog:
Rescue in Cougar Canyon

Adventures of Fraser the Yellow Dog:
Rescue at Maroon Bells

The World According to Fraser: A Memoir

The Blue Bottle, A Caribbean Adventure

Adventures of Kip in Aspen and Snowmass

Those Were The Days

Memories of an Aspen Hippie Chick

COURTNEY PRESS

COURTNEY PRESS

ISBN 978-0-9795592-3-5

Copyright © 2019 by Jill Sheeley

Published by COURTNEY PRESS · Aspen, Colorado

For more information about ordering books write:

Jill Sheeley, PO Box 845, Aspen CO 81612 · jillsheeleybooks.com

or email at: jillsheeleybooks@gmail.com

Cover Illustration by Amy Beidleman

Book Design & Layout by Marjorie DeLuca, Aspen Graphic Solultions, Inc.

Printed by Ingram Spark

This book is dedicated to Aspen,
the town that gave me a home.

Contents

*"We spend the
first 60 years of our lives
creating memories,
and the rest
trying to remember them."*

—JILL SHEELEY

Preface

While up in Canada on our favorite Gulf Island off Vancouver, I read a funny, informative, tongue-in-cheek book, *Adventures in Solitude* by Grant Lawrence. He writes about his family's crazy adventures beginning in the late 1970s building a cabin on a small, remote island in Desolation Sound, B.C. I read the first half of the book after kayaking to our favorite spot for a picnic and a little respite from the world.

The next day, even though a storm was predicted, my hubby Donnie and I took off for another paddle across the channel toward Wallace Island. We found a private island nearby with a fabulous sandy beach (most of the beaches up there are rocky and rough with oyster shells). We stayed only a short while as we felt the wind pick up. The sky darkened quickly and we watched as menacing white caps formed upon what had been a calm sea. We jumped into our boats and paddled against a strong current with cold, foamy waves crashing over the bow of our kayaks in this wild, unsettled and confused sea.

In these instances I go into a heightened state of focus and concentration. I need to put all my energy into paying attention. As a cold, relentless rain began, I paddled with conviction until, at last, we arrived safely at our take-out spot. We were soaked to the bone and chilled. After loading our kayaks on top of our car, we turned on the heat and drove back to our cottage in the woods. I made a roaring fire, a pot of hot coffee, propped up my feet and finished reading Grant's book.

I thought I really should write about my life in the '70s. Since I first arrived in Aspen in 1968, I'm kind of an old-timer. Why not me? Do I have stories to tell? You bet! In hindsight I've been telling them for years. It seemed apropos as I've been lucky enough to be an author since 1980. I've written a Christmas book; two cookbooks; a series of children's books about my yellow Lab, Fraser; Fraser's memoir; an Aspen-Caribbean novel;

3

and a children's book about my daughter's Australian shepherd, Kip.

I reflected on my life on that West Coast rainy afternoon and presto, an idea formed. When I get an idea, it's like a flash goes off and I literally run and grab my journal and start writing. The pen glides across the paper like my kayak when I'm paddling in the early mornings on flat water. I have no idea what I'm writing or why, but I just do it and it feels

great, and my wrist gets tired and I don't even mind.

I'll write a story about the town of Aspen and how she wooed me, then charmed me and then wove me into her fabric. I've been asked so many times: What was Aspen like in the '70s? I won't write a history book. I won't reinvent the wheel, as there are so many wonderful historical books that have already been written.

For me, Aspen is and always has been about the people—those who came to mine for silver, the anti-establishment, the doers, the ski bums, the hippies, the founding families, the movie stars, the dropouts, the dreamers, the artists, the musicians, the children, the athletes and the colorful characters who took hold of my spirit.

Years ago, my girlfriend and I were "skinning" up Aspen Mountain one early winter morning and I told her my idea of publishing a book about my yellow Lab, Fraser. I had already written it and was excited about the project. She asked me a fabulous question, "Do you think anyone will want to read it?"

Actually, I didn't have a clue but once I get the energy going, there's really no stopping me, so, even though her question was asked as a friend and gave me something to ponder, I published it. That book led to more books and opened many doors to me and fulfilled an unknown dream I didn't even know I had—to work with kids.

So, I started writing down my Aspen memories of the "good old days." I couldn't write fast enough. I knew I'd probably have to pop some Advil at night to ease my writer's arm and neck pain. I set out to tell my tale through the life and times of this amazing town I call home. We have our share of drama, we have triumphs, we have controversies, we have murders, and we have a huge circle of friends. We have the most caring community when tragedy falls, and it does way too often. I know this personally and am grateful for living here when it did. I believe above all, we live life to its fullest surrounded by these magnificent mountains.

After I returned home to Aspen and as I was enthusiastically writing down my memories, my current companion and yellow Lab, Ranger, would often lie down on my feet. I took this as a sign to keep going.

Waking Up in a Dream

So here goes: I came to Aspen my senior year, in 1968, with one of my best buddies. Kathy and I were fellow dreamers and took creative writing classes together in high school. Every afternoon, we'd walk a half hour from E.T.H.S. (Evanston Township High School) to a beach on Lake Michigan, sit on some rocks, take out our notebooks and write side by side. We didn't talk, we wrote and we were happy.

When I was young, I saw the Disney movie, *Little Skier's Big Day,* a 1959 movie produced and directed by local ski legend Fred Iselin. It's set in Aspen and is about a young girl (played by the real Susie Wirth) and her huge St. Bernard dog. The Wirth family actually lived on top of Aspen Mountain and ran the Sundeck restaurant at the time. The mostly true movie shows Susie skiing down the mountain every day to school. It's fun-filled with scenes of the town then—costume contests, skiers doing all sorts of tricks, and portraying a slow-paced ski town in the 1950s. One morning while skiing down the mountain to school, Susie is caught in a snowslide and her dog comes to the rescue. I loved that movie.

After seeing that impressionable film, I had dreams about going to Aspen to ski. In high school, I made my big brother take me up to Wilmot Mountain in Illinois to learn the sport. Wilmot was really just a hill, but it didn't take much to excite me. I rode up the slope on a rope tow (which put holes in my cheap gloves) and fell over again and again on my way down. My brother appropriately ditched me. I finally learned how to snowplow by watching others using lace-up leather boots and 210 cm skis that were way too tall for me at 5 foot, 4 inches. Even so, I was hooked.

I talked Kathy into a spring-break trip to Aspen. I was ready to tackle a real mountain (or so I thought). Our families didn't take spring-break vacations as many families do nowadays, so that trip had to be

earned by babysitting and mowing lawns as often as possible. There was no Internet to plan a trip—just a phone call to the Aspen Chamber of Commerce to find the cheapest room for two gals. We got a "package deal": A train ticket from Chicago to Denver, a bus ride up to Aspen, lift tickets, lodging at the hostel-style Dormez-Vous (on Durant Avenue across from Lift One Condos now called the Hotel Durant) and vouchers for breakfast and dinners—all this for under 300 dollars. Can you believe lift tickets were nine dollars a day?

We arrived in Aspen on a beautiful bluebird March day. I took one look at Aspen Mountain and knew, by hook or crook, I'd live here some-day. How could mountains have existed my entire seventeen years of life and I'd never seen one or experienced the size and sheer power? It was a true mystery that shortly after answered my dilemma of where to go to college.

Our week in Aspen was the very best week of my young life. I remember waking up early every morning at our hostel, walking out the door with my long skis carefully balanced on my shoulder, and looking up in a daze at the splendor of the mountain above me. It took my breath away. I was so excited to be going skiing day after day. It was perfect spring weather—sunny and warm. The two of us snowplowed even the steepest slopes but thought we were experts.

We met tons of "very cool" people from all over the world who also loved the carefree life of a skier. Our package included delicious, hearty breakfasts at the bustling Village Pantry, a local's favorite. They served the best eggs and hash browns I'd ever tasted. Dinners were at the ever-popular Skier's Chalet up the steep hill below Lift One. Owned and operated by Howard Awrey, the restaurant was a two-story old-style Swiss chalet where you waited outside for a table while drinking hot cider with fellow skiers and chatting about the ski day. My favorite memory is how the waitresses wheeled in a large wooden bowl of lettuce to our table and tossed it with each person's choice of salad dressing. It was unique, delicious and quite a show.

Each day was like waking up in a dream. I arrived back in Evanston with a "skier's sunburn" (complete with "raccoon eyes" from my sunglasses) and a totally new purpose in life—to attend the University of Denver, learn to be an awesome skier and move to Aspen. As I said before, when I set a goal, there's little stopping me.

A Sense of Place

My reality was turned upside down that week in Aspen. In Evanston, except for the lake, I felt no connection to the land, or to the history of the place. But when I finally did move to Aspen, I knew almost immediately this place held stories about people who came here in the 1800s in search of silver and a different life. They were gutsy and determined intrepid folks, enduring unknown hardships. It bred an unusual mentality, and I somehow felt connected.

I didn't expect to feel embraced by the local community but they wrapped their arms around me like I was an orphaned child. At home in Illinois my only mentors were wise relatives, but in Aspen so many individuals became mentors or looked out for me. I had never felt such a sense of place before.

In the fall of 1968, my parents sent me off on the train to Denver by myself for my first quarter at the University of Denver. I was beyond thrilled. That winter I hitchhiked every weekend to whatever ski area my ride took me—Loveland, Arapahoe Basin, Aspen, Winter Park, or Steamboat Springs. Aspen was my favorite because I could ski for free by working at the Merry-Go-Round—a funky cafeteria-style restaurant midway up Aspen Highlands. Pictures adorned the walls with Aspen ski legends, adding to the local flavor and making the place feel comfortable and homey. The owners, Freddie and Everett Peirce, were a young couple and two of the nicest people I'd ever met. They were fun-loving and hardworking, fulfilling a dream of raising their three children (Fred, Melanie and Tom) in a ski town. They came to Aspen in the '60s and also operated the Snowmass Lodge, a guest ranch located in the Snowmass Valley. Later they ran The Selway Lodge—a summer fishing guest resort located on the Selway River in Idaho. Everett flew supplies to their lodge in his plane. The guests rode horseback 15 miles one way to begin the adventure.

Those weekends in Aspen, I worked at the Merry-Go-Round during the lunch rush, skied the rest of the day, and always met people who let me "crash at their pads" for Friday and Saturday nights. Driving to and from Denver on I-70 was not what it is today. Not even close. First we had to navigate Loveland Pass which oftentimes was a dangerous, challenging road in the winter months. We drove two-way narrow highways and skirted constantly around rocks that had randomly fallen. The Eisenhower Tunnel had not been built yet—nowadays, folks take this covered, well-lit tunnel for granted. The nice four lanes through the Glenwood Canyon came much later, after a very long construction project that took years. Before that, the roads were treacherous—truly scary on blizzardy, snowy Sunday nights trying to make it back to Denver to sleep a few hours before my 8 o'clock sociology class on Monday mornings.

I had so many friends who were excellent skiers and didn't mind if I followed them down the slopes trying to figure out what they were doing—I had no money for ski lessons, which might have made my skiing career easier, but then looking back I'm glad I had to work for it.

It was hard because my expert friends made skiing look effortless, and I had no idea how they were doing it. One early morning after it had snowed a foot of champagne powder, I watched the ski patrol come down the mountain with their perfect S-turns and noticed how their arms bobbed up and down. I got to the top of the mountain full of confidence and took off skiing—really exaggerating bringing my arms up and down like they did. "This is it," I thought, "I've got it." But when I got down and looked up at my tracks, instead of perfect S-turns, there was one straight line. I still had a lot to learn but I was determined to enjoy the journey.

POPPY SEED CAKE

This recipe is from Freddie Peirce's cookbook
The Gourmet Woodburner.

1½ cup honey

¾ c margarine

1 tsp vanilla

4 eggs

1½ cups all-purpose flour

1½ cups whole-wheat flour

$^1/_3$ cup poppy seeds

2½ tsp baking soda

½ tsp salt

½ cup sour milk

$^1/_3$ cup mashed banana

½ cup raisins

powdered sugar

In a large bowl, thoroughly beat together the first three
ingredients until light and fluffy. Add eggs, one at a time
beating the mixture well after each addition.

Stir together the flours, poppy seeds, baking soda and salt.

Combine sour milk and mashed banana. Add dry ingredients
and sour milk mixture slternately, beating well after each
addition. Stir in raisins.

Turn onto a greased and floured 10" tube pan, spreading
batter evenly.

Bake at 350 degrees for 50-55 minutes or until it passes the
toothpick test. Cool cake in pan for 10 minutes. Invert onto
wire rack.

Cool cake completely and sprinkle with powdered sugar.

Love Changes All

My sophomore year in college I had hitchhiked up to Aspen for a week of skiing during a winter break. I was sitting down having lunch at the crowded Merry-Go-Round restaurant after my shift when this guy appeared still covered with snow. A blizzard was raging outside. He still had on his ski parka, hat and gloves and looked like a snowman! He asked if he could sit next to me (at one of the only available seats left). "Of course," I said.

He shook off the snow like a dog and all I could do was laugh, as now I was soaked too. He quickly apologized. Pulling off his wet hat and goggles, I noticed how cute he was—brown hair, a thick mustache, kind brown eyes and a great, wide smile that lit up the room.

We fell into easy conversation. He said his name was Mike. I told him that I was an aspiring ski bum, and he said he worked at the Red Onion at night so that he could ski all day. I listened intently as he explained how ski bumming worked for him. We met that evening at The Slope—a clever name for a large, sloped, carpeted seating area on the floor (like nothing I've seen since) located in the basement of the Aspen Mine Company on the Hyman Avenue Mall. They showed continuous free ski movies and cartoons and served food and drinks. After the movies, Mike and I talked some more and got to know each other. I felt the butterflies in my stomach when I was with Mike. I met his friends and liked them all.

We had an amazing week—we skied all day together, and at night Mike played the guitar jamming with friends by a roaring fire. It was all too good to be true. I was high on what life could be like in this special mountain town. I was hit by a feeling that would entice me and lure me back. This feeling had true power over me. I felt rooted. I felt at home. Mike and I quickly fell in love. I believe it was fate. Being in love with a great guy who shared my free and adventuresome spirit was more than I expected. I tried to get to Aspen as often as possible that winter. Life couldn't have been better.

Besides Mike, I had another new love: The mountains surrounding Aspen made me want to get up early each day to absorb the enormously happy feeling and lock it in somehow. Even the quality of the light offered me such clarity of purpose. I did not feel this in Denver and for sure not in Evanston.

One spring day back at the wonderful University of Denver, I was sitting in some class, daydreaming out the window when it hit me like a ton of bricks—*I could actually move to Aspen*. I was studying sociology and loved it, but suddenly realized it was not going to lead me to a career I'd be passionate about. I was working two jobs for extra cash, but my heart was in Aspen. I decided then and there to move to Aspen, spend the summer with Mike, go back to school for fall quarter, go back to Aspen for the winter and pursue my career of becoming a ski bum. My immature logic was: Certainly I could create a career—or at the least, I could work several jobs to survive—right?

Still, I had a few months left to be a college student. I was living in a great little house near campus. My good friend and roommate Margaret and I were shopping at Albertson's one fateful afternoon when we spotted a cute, pig-tailed, eight-year-old girl holding a sign saying: *Please adopt these pups or my mom will take them to a shelter TODAY!* Our compassion and impulsiveness got the better of us, and we cuddled the last two mutts in the litter. We loved them within seconds. I named my adorable brown and white puppy Brandy. She became my best friend.

The small grey and white house Margaret and I lived in didn't have a fenced-in yard so we immediately understood the fact that having two wild puppies was going to be a challenge. We'd have to leave them inside most of the day and when they weren't sleeping, they loved to demolish the rugs and the furniture. They especially loved to pull apart the trash in the bathroom—get the picture? We built a fence a couple of days later with the help of some frat boys.

I began taking Brandy to my classes, where I was surprisingly met with accommodating and dog-loving professors.

Freedom

School ended in the spring and I packed my Girl Scout canvas backpack with essential items. I had 126 dollars in cash—money saved from dishing out ice cream and flipping burgers at the Student Union. Brandy and I got a ride to Highway I-25 so we could hitch a ride to Aspen. It took us only three rides by kind people to arrive in Glenwood Springs where we were enthusiastically met by Mike and his black Lab Barney in Mike's vintage blue 1962 Volkswagen bus.

As we drove out of Glenwood, I could see the regal, snow-covered Sopris Mountain and large vivid green fields below where millions of bright yellow dandelions grew. I instantly knew I was coming home.

We parked our "home" on Durant Avenue next to Wagner Park that evening so Mike could work his night shift at the infamous Red Onion where he waited tables four nights a week. I couldn't believe when he told me the Red Onion (formerly the Brick Saloon) was built in 1892 and back then had a brothel upstairs. Very juicy. Very old. Owned and operated by Swiss chef Werner Kuster, the Red Onion was a gathering spot for locals and tourists. One side of the restaurant was an elegant dining room serving gourmet cuisine and the other side was a nightclub hosting the likes of Billie Holiday and local saxophone player and jazz favorite Freddy Fisher ("Freddy the Fixer").

Mike made great tips and would return back to the bus with enough leftover meat scraps and bones (people ate a lot more meat in those days) to allow Brandy and Barney to eat like royalty. It will gross you out, and believe me, it grosses me out now, but Mike and I "dined" on customers' leftovers, too. Say what you will, we were young and broke and these leftovers were succulent, delicious and free.

That first summer in Aspen was magic. If I had returned to Evanston, I would have had my old job back. I would have woken up at 5:30 a.m.

and driven 45 minutes to a nursing home where I worked as a physical therapy aide. I actually loved that job; I adored my patients and my mentor, Mrs. Johnson (the head PT), who could easily lift a 300-pound man all while telling dirty jokes. Plus, I wore an adorable little nurse's outfit my high school boyfriend said made me look sexy!

Instead, I was living the life. Little me, who had never done anything extraordinary was living in the mountains, in Aspen, and was truly free for the first time. Mike and I moved the bus every weekend to a different spot outside of town so we could hike with the dogs and discover new trails. After walking several hours, we were rewarded with spectacular vistas. I loved watching the dogs sniff everything and joyously jump into streams and rivers to swim and drink the clear water. Mountain wildflowers were a new concept, and I kept a little journal to write and record the descriptions of the flowers so later I could find out what they were: Colorado blue columbines (our state flower), fireweed, primrose, lupine, iris, Indian paintbrush and a million others. Mike had a vase in his bus which I filled with a combination of these wildflowers and put on our tiny camping table to add to the ambiance.

After the hike, we'd come back to the bus, read, make dinner and then sit by the fire while Mike played his 12-string guitar under the stars. We'd wake up to the birds singing vigorously, a nearby river's comforting sound and the special reward of being in this place—just the two of us and our dogs. For a girl who grew up in a busy neighborhood, this peace and quiet was so new to me and yet I knew it would become something I wanted more of. It would become the fabric of my life.

Mike and I would slowly sip coffee, look at his map and take off for yet another incredible day of discovering everything these mountains had to offer. Many afternoons we'd come back to the bus laughing, starving and sunburned. Who knew anything about SPF sunscreen in those days? Heck, we doused ourselves with greasy Bain de Soleil or baby oil mixed with iodine to get lots of color. After an adventurous day, sometimes toasting marshmallows was enough for dinner.

What truly astounded me about being in the mountains at night was the abundance of stars, so close I felt I could touch them. We'd lie down and watch the falling stars and keep track of who saw the most. I'd catch them and put them in my pocket for good luck. If we were lucky enough to have a full moon, it was the frosting on the best cake you've ever tasted. Those days and nights taught me what true happiness is.

Sunday afternoons, we'd pack up and drive back to town for another workweek, relaxed and refreshed. One day, hanging out in Wagner Park embroidering yet another muslin peasant blouse to add to my tiny wardrobe, a very tall, well-dressed man came up to me and introduced himself as Charlie Knight. He asked if I knew how to bead as well as embroider. He must have noticed my hundreds of strands of colored embroidery threads along with my coveted collection of Indian beads lying on my blanket.

Yes, I told him I'd been teaching myself the craft of beading for the past year. Charlie told me he owned a high-end shop called Country Flower and was looking for someone to bead the cuffs and collars of chamois shirts that would be custom-sewn and sold to wealthy tourists, movie stars and musicians searching for something uniquely Western. Yes, I said, I'd love to try. He asked when I could start. We worked out a few details and I followed him to the shop on Hyman Avenue, got some sample pieces and started that same day. It was perfect. I couldn't wait to tell my parents I had already landed a job.

My parents had lived through the Depression and my dad never finished high school. However, he had a great work ethic and worked his way up from errand boy to vice president of media in a prestigious advertising agency in Chicago. He also taught media at Northwestern University, which was a coup as it allowed us three kids to use their amazing sports facilities—especially the new ice-skating rink. He worked hard, learned along the way and had that can-do attitude. His goal was to send all three of us kids to college. My parents owned a small house and lived frugally.

Looking back, my adult self can only imagine my parents' looks of disbelief after sending their daughter to college just to find out she was "beading" and living in a VW bus. Certain things in those days I simply kept to myself.

Charlie Knight, owner of Country Flower, ca 1970s

Little did they know I'd be hitchhiking up Independence Pass with Brandy every day to either the Grottos or the Devil's Punchbowl. I'd lay out a blanket with my current project and bead for hours. They were my parents, and of course they'd never understand, so I sort of sugar-coated my endeavors. I certainly didn't need for them to worry. My older brother had already outdone me. Although he had finished college, he sported super long hair, grew a scraggly beard, wore overalls and was building a geodesic dome in Northern (as in Garberville) California with several other hippies. Naked children were running around the woods and the smell of marijuana permeated the air. You should have seen when my parents went to visit him!

Up the pass, Brandy loved playing in the water with all the other dogs. I met tons of young people just hanging out, smoking pot and sunning themselves on the hot rock formations. It was incredible to see all these uninhibited, naked hippies. I was from Illinois where no one laid out naked on any of the beaches I frequented. Comical, shocking, eye-popping—yes, all of the above. I bet the skin docs were observing from behind a tree rubbing their hands together knowing how much money they'd eventually make off us kids who didn't wear sunscreen and literally worshipped the Colorado sunshine.

I finally let loose of my inhibitions that summer when we journeyed to the soothing natural waters of the Penny Hot Springs near Redstone. We'd heard it was amazing—one of the locals' best-kept secrets. The steamy waters were dammed with river rocks, creating private pools. It was evening and a full moon. I kept a towel around my naked, skinny, shivering body, making sure no one was looking. I quickly made a mad dash to the river, shedding my towel at the water's edge. After the first few embarrassing plunges, it became second nature. We visited the Penny Hot Springs often. Still, I didn't go totally "native" and continued to bead, wearing my cut-off blue jean shorts and my skimpy, handmade halter tops.

Ten miles up Independence Pass is the Devil's Punchbowl where I spent a lot of time that fateful summer. High stone cliffs rise hundreds of feet from the river below and it's spectacular. When you arrive by the road from town, you're at the top of these cliffs, so looking down into the water is mesmerizing. The roar of the rushing water is powerful. Small waterfalls feed into a narrowing in the river to make it all the more dramatic with the churning whitewater.

In those days, not many daring souls attempted to jump from the top. Mike was an accomplished diver and blew everyone's minds by diving, yes, diving headfirst and then adding dazzling tricks to the show. Tourists would stop and stand in awe of this young man who risked life and limb for the rush of a lifetime.

Did I mention how freaking cold it is? I realized within a day or two I could experience my own mini rush by jumping from the lower ledge. On impact, it was so cold my entire body went numb—it wasn't until I screamed at the top of my lungs that I was able to swim to the nearest rock to get out as quickly as possible. Those gutsy plunges taught me the true meaning of an ice-cream headache.

Age of Aquarius

Most of us 20-year-olds (and I tread lightly here) in Aspen in the summer of 1970 were hippies to one degree or another. NEWS FLASH—not everyone liked hippies. Even though Aspen had a wonderful laissez-faire attitude for the most part, there was a segment of folks who disliked, disapproved or even despised us. A case in point was Guido Meyer, who owned Guido's restaurant. He was a stern European man who had no time or love for hippies. He placed a sign at his restaurant saying, "No Hippies Allowed." And he meant it.

The legendary story that was told to me (and I'm not saying it was true) goes something like this: One night Guido was having dinner at the Red Onion and in walked two long-haired hippies. For no reason, Guido threw a glass bottle of catsup at one of the poor guys. The bottle hit the guy in the face and he was pretty badly hurt. He took Guido to court and when the judge asked him why he threw the bottle, Guido calmly replied, "I could have sworn the guy asked me to pass the catsup."

Even before I came to town, in 1967 Guido was on a mission to free Aspen of all hippies. Being the local magistrate, he persuaded the police to arrest hippies for any minor offense. A young hitchhiker was arrested and sentenced to 90 days in jail. Can you imagine?

Joe Edwards, a longtime local attorney who at the age of 28 represented one of these "hippies," remembers Guido saying in court, "Those dirty hippies. They're all over the place, and they're filthy and they haven't washed, and they smoke dope."

Edwards became known as the "hippie lawyer" and gained the respect of our very own outspoken and colorful Hunter S. Thompson. He convinced Edwards to run for mayor, but Edwards was beaten by Eve Homeyer (Aspen's first woman mayor!) by just six votes.

I was thankful that by the time I arrived in Aspen three years later, things had relaxed. I can remember Mike and me sitting outside our VW bus one beautiful evening with a few friends smoking pot. Two young policemen walked by, and I was too stoned to run or really care that we might get busted. Instead of arresting us, the cops noticed Mike's 12-string guitar and asked if he'd play a few tunes. They were super bored. Oh, I knew I loved this town, but that night, "chillin' out" took on a whole new meaning.

We had no computers, no Internet, no cell phones, no TV. I know this sounds super sappy and archaic but life really was different then. I used to roll my eyes when my grandparents described their lives at the turn of the century. But here it is many decades later and I can only imagine my grandkids rolling their eyes that we existed without video games, Twitter, Instagram, Facebook, email, hashtags and a zillion other new things that have come to pass in my lifetime.

Joe Edwards, the "Hippie Lawyer"

DEFINITION OF A "HIPPIE"
BECAUSE I WAS ONE

For those of you too young to really understand the term "hippie," I'll do my best to give you my personal definition.

First, there was the "look."

Guys—had long hair but not dreadlocks, wore cut-off, frayed blue jeans with a T-shirt proclaiming a ski brand or a favorite music group and wore funky, worn sandals.

Girls—had long hair worn in braids or pigtails, wore peasant tops, halter tops, bathing suit tops, cut-off frayed blue jean shorts and flip-flops. Yes, it's true, a flower was oftentimes tucked behind an ear just like the hippie chicks of Haight Ashbury. No bras, no makeup and no such thing as going to a hair stylist.

Second, there was a gentle, loving attitude toward your fellow man. Live and let live. Play as often as possible, listen to lots of music, dance and be free. Only work as much as needed in order to pay the rent, feed your pet and have a little left over for groceries.

Ski Addict

The relaxed and warm breezy summer ended abruptly for me. I turned in my last beaded project to Charlie with pride. One minute it was June and I was hanging out in town, treating myself to a delicious coffee ice-cream cone from the soda fountain at Carl's Pharmacy and the next minute fall was in the air and DU was back in session. Mike and I had already made a plan. As soon as the fall quarter was over (before Christmas) I'd be back in Aspen. Even Brandy was sad to leave our little mountain town and the laid-back lifestyle.

One sunny fall weekend Brandy and I and my good friend and college roommate Marion (Mare) drove to Aspen to see Mike and go hiking. The aspen trees had turned many brilliant shades of gold with some patches of reds and oranges. Mare and I were both from the Midwest and were mesmerized by the metamorphosis of colors of the aspen trees. We were used to oaks and maples. Fall in the Midwest brought back memories of raking millions of leaves and then rolling in the piles and backyard leaf-burning with that distinctive smell.

John Short, Mike's best friend from childhood (we called him either Short John or Short), was a tall, blond-haired, super friendly guy with a great laugh and mustache. He moved to Aspen in hopes of getting on the Aspen Highlands ski patrol. Short and Mare hit if off immediately. Soon after, we hatched our newest plan: The four of us would live together in a two-bedroom trailer in El Jebel the boys had just found. I promised Mare we'd go back to DU for spring quarter. I was pretty persuasive in those days.

Our tiny blue-and-white trailer was located all by itself behind where Bella Mia restaurant is currently located. We all worked different jobs with various schedules. I went back to work at Aspen Highlands for Freddie and Everett Peirce at the Merry-Go-Round, obtaining my first ski pass, and allowing me time to improve my skiing.

Mare had skied her whole life and was a great skier. I followed her down all the ski trails and emulated her style. Sometimes it snowed all day long for three or four days straight. This was so new to me as, of course, this never happened in Evanston. It was incredible to wake up after these mountain storms dumped several feet of fresh powder snow. Virgin white snow against bright blue skies—it couldn't be better. Skiing powder takes a whole other skill set—one I was determined to learn because I loved the feeling of this light snow flying in my face. There's a freedom in skiing I'd never felt before. I was addicted.

One of the highlights of the winter happened one day when I was finally able to ski effortlessly down a slope. I spotted a young girl who had fallen and was way behind her ski instructor, who was below with the rest of the class. She was wailing. I stopped to help her get up. I collected her hat, goggles, ski poles, dusted her off and calmed her down. I asked her name and gave her a quick hug. Then I skied back down with her to her grateful instructor. Out of nowhere, a tall man skied up to me. He introduced himself as "Lefty" (Brinkman). He explained he was head of the Highlands' Ski School and had watched me help out the little

Jeff Harp, Cone-making Champion from Corpus Christi, Texas, Shown on the Job at Carl's Pharmacy.

Carl's Pharmacy Soda Fountain

girl who had fallen. He asked if I'd like a job teaching skiing the following season. This was too good to be true. Yes, I said quickly, I'd love to and floated on air the rest of the day.

DEFINITION OF A SKI BUM
IN THE "OLD DAYS"

Sorry to burst your bubble, guys, but now we have maybe one or two true ski bums left in town. I no longer qualify. But in the '60s and '70s, I'd say the definition of a ski bum was quite different than it is today:

1. We had no trust fund and no source of extra money—many times arriving with $20 in our pockets.

2. We resented those who claimed to be ski bums but actually had hidden sources and didn't suffer from the stress of being able to stay here.

3. Many of us had no possessions except skis, boots, poles and a few items of clothing.

4. Our driving force was skiing—we lived and breathed it.

5. We ski bums shared a bond.

6. We shopped at the fabulous Cheap Shots, the first consignment store in Aspen, and the only affordable place for locals. Owned and operated by the talented and hardworking Julie Wyckoff, it was the best deal in town.

I Didn't See It Coming

Winter in Aspen, with the shortened days, was so different than summer. By the time work and skiing were done, we were so exhausted, we went home, made and ate dinner, shared stories of the day and fell sound asleep. Mike hardly played his guitar. I didn't have a car and Mike, Short, Mare and I had very different schedules. More often than not, I hitchhiked to and from Aspen Highlands. The bus system was not what it is now. I loved the winter and yet it had its challenges. That winter presented me with a twist I could never have predicted.

A year before, in December 1969, the Vietnam draft lottery became a reality. During those days and weeks, many a son volunteered to fight in Vietnam and many declared, "No way," no matter what number they were assigned. Many devised plans to escape to Canada, many used college deferments, some faced imprisonment and burned their draft cards and many, like Mike, who had a low number, stressed out about the situation, knowing they didn't want to go to war—especially this one.

A dark cloud hovered over boys, their families and their loved ones. It was a highly charged time for all of us. We were all affected by this possible inevitable non-choice to serve a war most people I knew didn't believe in. I remember sitting around my family's breakfast table—my parents supporting my brother's decision that if he was drafted he would escape to Canada. He was lucky—he didn't have to. My cousin did.

Short had a high lottery number but he and Mike discussed Mike's options extensively as they were blood brothers and would do anything for each other. Mike and several other draftees from the Pitkin County area were bused to Denver to a draft office for a pre-induction physical. Mike did everything in his power (like so many others) to flunk his tests with flying colors. These young men were sent home to worry whether or not they had been selected for active duty. Mike kept most of this stress and anxiety to himself or discussed it in length with Short or his other buddies.

Most of my family and friends opposed the Vietnam War. The year 1968 marked Lyndon B. Johnson's fifth year as Commander in Chief and was the deadliest single year of the war, 19,000 Americans—dead, 170,000 Vietnamese—dead. There were protests around the country. At DU we set up "Woodstock West" on the lawn by the Student Union. Classes were boycotted. Tents were erected. We protested not only the war in Vietnam, but also the recent invasion of Cambodia by LBJ's successor, President Richard Nixon. Because the war was televised, we were shocked at the killing of innocent men, women and children by napalm in remote villages far from home. But it wasn't a million miles away, it was on TVs in living rooms around the country and we saw the carnage with our own eyes. They couldn't hide the truth from us—even though in so many ways they did.

We mourned the killing of four innocent students at Kent State and the wounding of nine others. Emotions were stirred up like a cyclone. We were all frenzied. We all wanted to be a part of a movement that said "no" to the establishment. We were tired of the government sending innocent young men (really just boys) to a war we didn't believe in. Hell, no. We'd had enough.

In looking back now I so respected all who served our country. It was terribly painful to have us so divided. Nowadays I go to every Memorial Day celebration here in Aspen and cry at the losses. I can't imagine what those poor boys coming home went through, with their war scars and their anger.

Then there was the music. Music energized us. Bob Dylan, Pete Seeger, Joan Baez, Peter, Paul and Mary sang to us of ending wars. College musicians sang these songs in solidarity. Speeches were made by educated people and riled us up. We were totally together on this task.

And here was Mike, my boyfriend, personally caught up in the reality of having no say over what the government was telling him he must do. On top of that, he had a rigid and overbearing father who didn't like his long hair (in comparison, it was hardly considered long) and his lifestyle. When I'd ask Mike about his family, he never talked about them. He laughed it off and told me his father had disowned him. He didn't want or need his father's one-sided judgment. He had no photos to show me of his family. I accepted this, as I was only 19 years young. I talked about my family all the time but I, too, didn't miss home.

I never sensed Mike's anxiety growing. I never saw the storm brewing. But somewhere, somehow during the winter, I believe Mike became obsessed with the clear fact he did not want to fight in Vietnam and might not be able to stop the process. In hindsight, it must have been a rough winter for him—not knowing his outcome and keeping it all in. I should have noticed it in his eyes or in the slump of his shoulders, but I did not.

So many died fighting in Vietnam and some slowly died in their own private war.

Winter season was nearing the end. Mare and I were sadly packing to go back to college. Days later, my world would fall apart. I vividly remember walking into our trailer with Mare and Short. Brandy dashed behind the couch and wouldn't come out. I remember thinking, "What the hell is going on?" Mare and Short told me sheepishly that Mike had been kicking Brandy for no reason and that whenever the door opened, she ran for cover. They both felt terrible they didn't stop it nor did they tell me what was happening. They felt torn. They thought it would end.

I was shocked beyond belief that Mike was capable of hurting even a flea. This was my beloved dog. How could he? I wished he had kicked me instead. I felt betrayed by a guy I thought I truly loved. From then on, I made sure Brandy was never alone with Mike. I even took her into the bathroom with me and locked the door. I moved onto the couch.

Lost

Very soon after, Marion and I went back to DU for the spring quarter. Mike and Barney came down on weekends. Mike apologized constantly (don't they all?) and said it would never happen again. Brandy stayed away from him and knew I'd protect her. Mike was back to his old self: nice, sweet, fun. I was wary, careful, confused and disillusioned. I was naïve, but then I was so young and had never known abuse could happen in my world. I hadn't grown up with people who did a 180 as Mike had. If those poor, young soldiers going to Nam were clueless of what awaited them, then so was I on a different front.

Life continues on and spring in Denver is joyful with warm days, flowers sprouting out of their winter homes and leaves returning to the bare trees. The parks are brimming with energy—kids playing, dogs exploring. Life is new and inviting. The spring of my life brought new revelations. I'd quit school for good. My sociology major was always interesting but I knew I didn't want to be a social worker. To graduate, I'd have to go four more quarters and I was beginning to feel penned in. I'd had a taste of the life of a ski bum and loved it. I longed to be back in Aspen. Surely my parents would get over it with time.

As soon as I finished spring exams, I sold my schoolbooks, packed up my meager belongings and hitchhiked with Brandy up to Aspen. Mike and I seemed to be in a good place. Mike had a few days off work so we planned a backpacking trip to Capitol Lake before I started working again.

I had hiked a lot but had never packed everything for several days in a backpack that I'd need to carry for nearly 13 miles roundtrip. All I had was an old Girl Scout backpack that didn't have a supporting frame. Mike carried our food, tent and other essentials. I learned quickly that when I got back to Aspen and started working, I'd be saving up for proper gear.

A good friend drove us at the crack of dawn to the trailhead down the Snowmass Creek Road—five miles of pavement and three miles on a dirt road—a journey in itself. For me, the hike was difficult because I wasn't yet acclimated. However, we walked through aspen groves, lovely meadows and spruce forests that made me take my mind off my sore feet and instead enjoy the amazing scenery. I felt in total harmony with a force bigger than myself—I was learning about spirituality.

Capitol Lake is stunningly beautiful and it was worth all the hard work to get there. I was covered in sweat. When we finally arrived I quickly dropped my backpack and jumped into the freezing cold but welcoming water. The lake is set beneath the majestic and massive West Face of Capitol Peak, rising to 14,130 feet. When Mike told me experienced climbers summited the peak, I was awestruck. Over the years, many experienced climbers perished on that mountain and unfortunately, still do.

We spent four wonderful days in the quiet serenity by this pristine mountain lake. I was so content and loved being there with no other people anywhere nearby. Brandy and Barney explored and played endlessly until they could no longer stay awake.

One beautiful, sunny afternoon, Brandy and I ventured off on a hike. I brought my journal and pen. We walked for hours and stopped by a stream for a rest—a perfect place to write and reflect. We got up and hiked another hour. I wasn't paying close enough attention and soon realized I was hopelessly lost.

I had never been alone before on a mountain trail that far from a home base. I was turned around and had no idea what to do. I was wearing cut-off jeans and a halter top. I had no extra layers, no food nor water and I was beginning to freak out. The temperature was dropping rapidly and when I looked up I couldn't believe I hadn't noticed dark storm clouds collecting above. I could feel my heart beating loudly.

I looked at Brandy and asked her frantically to get us back to camp. I just knew she knew the way. She was, after all, a dog, and had a great sense of smell and direction and I was an unprepared, foolish girl. "Lead the way and I will trust and follow you."

Booming thunder was close by followed by flashes of lightning. How

did I get so lost? I knew I was in trouble with this storm coming in quickly.

Brandy wagged her tail in circles and took off down a path I never would have chosen. We hiked for what seemed like eternity. It started pouring rain. The raindrops were relentless and hurt my exposed skin. Soon I was shivering, but luckily we never stopped and the walking kept me warmer than I expected. I was soaked to the bone and caked with mud.

I was so exhausted, nothing mattered but finding our way back. The rain finally let up. There was still a short time before it would be completely dark. Then, I saw the rock cairn I had admired earlier in the day at the beginning of our journey. It felt like days since we took off. I knew we were near our camp and rejoiced when I saw our tent in the distance.

I learned the first of many outdoor lessons that day. I truly believe Brandy saved me. If I had gone the way I originally thought was correct, I'm sure I would have spent a very cold, wet evening out in the elements hugging poor Brandy for warmth. I know I wouldn't have died, but being rescued was not something I would have ever asked for.

Mike was genuinely sick with worry over where we'd been. He warmed me up and sang me to sleep. Brandy fell sound asleep by my side, snoring softly.

I slept for ten hours like a dead person. I spent the next day close to camp drying out my clothes and hiking boots in anticipation of leaving the following day. We packed up and hiked the long way back, blisters and all. Mike had to be back at 5 p.m., showered and ready to work at the Red Onion.

All was well—I had survived my first scary, out-of-control backcountry experience and it was a perfect, sunny day. Mike and I hiked at an easy pace, not needing to talk. And just like that, there was a life-changing moment. Brandy got in front of Mike. He kicked her gently and said, "Get going, lame dog." That was the crystal clear moment. It was my moment and it didn't take another second for me to decide. After all the effort, after a lovely spring together, I realized as sure as the sun rises in the east, Mike and I were done. He hadn't done anything to Brandy in months but be kind to her. What I realized on the mountain that day was that Mike was not to be trusted and I couldn't live like that—never knowing when he might strike again.

I didn't say a word. He turned around and apologized. We got back to town, he went to work and I packed my few possessions once again and left a note telling him we were over. I called a friend and asked if I could crash on her couch for a while.

Forgiveness

A year later, Mike would be dead. He spent the following summer in 1972 in Montauk, Long Island, working at a restaurant. The last night before he was to come back to Aspen, his "buddies" coaxed him into partying with them. Mike wasn't a drinker—he smoked pot but didn't like hard liquor. He was an athlete. The story that was told to me was tragic. Peer pressure got to him and he drank way too much. He went to bed, vomited, aspirated and, boom, a life was taken too early.

It was my first jolt of dealing with death. I was sad for his family (whom I'd never met) and for Short John and for Barney. I didn't go to Iowa for his funeral. I wrote his parents a condolence card with a note leaving out the obvious.

I finally accepted the sad truth that Mike was possessed by discontentment and hidden anger. He might have been a willing participant (without knowing it) when death came calling. I'll never know.

Years later, I forgave Mike and here is what I wrote.

Mike was a young man, full of hopes and dreams. He had been a dutiful son, brother, cousin, friend. He led a normal life in a conventional Midwestern town with a traditional family. After doing everything expected of him, he felt a strong, burning desire to live in the mountains of Colorado with his black Lab, Barney, and his best friend, Short John. Sometimes burning desires can truly ignite when you least expect it. Sometimes a perfect full moonlit evening with a million stars can fade to nothing. Sometimes, the brilliant moon and stars can vanish with the blink of an eye. Sometimes an unjustified war a million miles away can come along and ruin your perfect life.

I wished Mike peace in his afterlife. His betrayal had come to me in disguise. Forgiveness was the only way for me to live.

Life Goes On

It was June 1971. I had no job, no place to live and no boyfriend. But I had an open mind and a passion for living in Aspen. I slept on friends' couches for a couple of nights before I heard through the grapevine that some psychologists were coming to Aspen to live for two months and were looking for a "house girl" to cook and clean while they took continuing education classes. In exchange, they'd supply a room at the Aspen Alps. I interviewed and got the job.

Brandy and I moved into our little room the next day. What a coup—all I had to do was cook gourmet vegetarian dinners for four kind men. One quarter at DU, I shared a house with a couple who had owned a vegetarian restaurant in Indiana. They had taught me enough to fulfill this nightly project of cooking and experimenting with ingredients.

The guys made sure I sat down and ate with them. What a bonus. They loved Brandy, as they missed their dogs from home and would sometimes take her hiking when they had time off. We had very interesting conversations about their profession and their patients. I learned a lot from them. Hilarious jokes were always a big part of the dining experience.

I enjoyed poring over cookbooks I found at a local bookstore and begged recipes from several restaurant owners and chefs. Creating tasty and healthy meals was always my goal. When the guys interviewed me, they told me to cook whatever I wanted. They confessed they were all used to meat and potatoes but after a few dinners, they really learned to savor the surprisingly delicious and unusual combination of veggies, rice and cheeses. They welcomed my Baked Acorn Squash filled with veggies and bread crumb stuffing, my Mushroom Burgers and my Veggie Strudel. They hounded me weekly to make Moussaka after they tried this mouth-watering eggplant dish. I packed them Cinnamon Oatmeal Cookies for snacks and they devoured all my desserts—Sour Cream Orange Cake was their all-time favorite.

I continued to "bead" for Charlie (Knight) at Country Flower. I had all day to myself before beginning dinner around 4 p.m. Being unattached was a revelation. I met so many young people every day via the Aspen network. We hiked and explored together by day and I was invited to impromptu parties at night after I made and served dinner to my "guys." That summer was fun and casual. My broken heart was beginning to heal.

VEGGIE MOUSSAKA

3 medium eggplants, sliced
and salted

3 zucchini, sliced

3 large potatoes, sliced

3 cloves of garlic, roasted

1 onion, diced

2 cans (15 ounces) diced
tomotoes

3 T chopped fresh dill

1 tsp oregano

½ cup Parmesan, grated

½ cup breadcrumbs

2½ cups warm milk

3 T flour

¼ cup butter

1 egg, beaten

olive oil

salt, pepper, nutmeg

Bake sliced zucchini on an oiled pan in oven at 425 degrees for 15 minutes. Bake the sliced potatoes, then eggplant in the same manner. Put aside.

In a large frying pan, heat some olive oil and sauté the onion. Then add garlic and diced tomatoes and cook for 10 minutes.

Make the sauce: melt the butter over low heat, whisk in the flour to make a roux. Whisk in the warm milk and cook until fairly thick. Beat in the egg.

Use parchment paper or butter a casserole dish. Cover the bottom with eggplant, sprinkle with breadcrumbs and grated cheese, use ½ the tomato sauce, then add the potatoes and zucchinis, sprinkle with more breadcrumbs and grated cheese and the rest of the tomato sauce. Top with the sauce and sprinkle with the remaining breadcrumbs and cheese.

Bake at 350 degrees covered for 40 minutes and then an extra 15 minutes uncovered. Serve with a green salad.

A New Love

One day I was cutting through the driveway of The Glory Hole lodge (formerly the Sky Hotel and now W Aspen) when I ran into my girlfriend Giz. We were chatting and she spotted a white Jeep in the driveway. She grabbed me by my arm and we ran over to the Jeep where a guy sat petting his Irish setter. Strangely, Brandy jumped right into the Jeep. This was

unusual, as she didn't like men anymore. Giz introduced me to Donnie and his beautiful Irish setter Killy and abruptly took off to go to her job.

Donnie was cute. When he smiled his lip tried to cover a chipped front tooth, but you could see it and I liked it. He had on frayed blue jean shorts and a Rossignol T-shirt. He wore a multicolored headband around his thick blond head of hair. I noticed he was very tan, lean and yet well sculpted and toned. He seemed different from all the guys I had met that summer. He had a little hippie and a little Old School prep in his appearance—I can't explain it. Little did I know that starched Brooks Brothers shirts would become one of his trademarks years later.

I was tired after an all-day hike so I popped into his open-air Jeep. Donnie and I began chatting like we'd known each other forever. Donnie didn't want to fight in Vietnam so he joined the Peace Corps and was sent to San José, Costa Rica, where he was immersed in a Spanish language class. From there he was sent to a small town on the Caribbean side. He thought he was going there to help save the world, but when he was placed at a desk job in a bank, he was disappointed, unimpressed and restless. He traveled to the Caribbean beaches on weekends, fished with the locals and set up an underwater marine park for snorkeling. While in Costa Rica he was misdiagnosed with Pink Eye, which ironically got him out of the draft. He came home speaking fluent Spanish with many tales to tell. He and his sister Bev moved from Illinois to Aspen to do what we were all doing—enjoying a life in the mountains. Turns out, we'd grown up 45 minutes away from each other.

I'd see him almost every day after that fateful meeting. He taught sailing for the City of Aspen at Ruedi Reservoir. In the afternoons he'd lay out all the sails on the grass and hose them off and I'd help him fold them as Killy and Brandy chased tennis balls.

Donnie and I spent the summer together as buddies—hiking, jeeping and sailing. I had never jeeped before and loved getting to remote places and hiking from there. Killy and Brandy became instant best dog buddies. Killy, better known as Killy Four-Wheelie, was a very sweet dog but it never ceased to amaze me that every time I looked at him sitting regally in the front seat of the Jeep, he had two long strings of slobber

coming from both sides of his mouth.

Donnie and I would cycle partway up Independence Pass in the full moon, which was an experience I looked forward to every month. I felt as if we were on the moon and not under it. There was no evening traffic back then. We spent many nights camping in new spots and chatting endlessly by a blazing campfire.

Sailing

My first time driving to Ruedi Reservoir with Donnie was yet another revelation. We drove past the little town of Basalt, up the two-lane twisty road that follows the Gold Medal fly-fishing waters of the Frying Pan River. I noticed many fishermen standing in the water all decked out for fly-fishing for trout. I wondered how they could stand there for hours until I understood their passion many years later.

Thirteen miles up the road we arrived at the reservoir—a large, sparkling lake surrounded by mountains. More than once deer crossed the road unimpressed by us. I spotted a family of foxes. We drove another five miles around the lake and turned onto the Aspen Yacht Club road which was a dirt road that traveled a couple of miles downhill to the lake. I fell in love immediately as I missed being by water. Growing up, Lake Michigan was practically in my backyard. Donnie told me about Aspen architect and legend Fritz Benedict who had donated the land to the Yacht Club due to his passion for sailing. I later met Fritz—he was a kind and generous gentleman and truly gifted in his field and had studied with Frank Lloyd Wright.

My only sailing experience had been in high school when my girl-friends and I snuck into the Wilmette Yacht Club and got ourselves invited by cute guys on their beautiful sailboats. Sailing a small boat on Ruedi Reservoir is exciting as the winds are fluky and sometimes violent, which oftentimes leads to wild rides. I met old-time locals at the Aspen Yacht Club—a spiffy name for a shack and a beach.

I knew skiers were competitive, but I had no idea that sailors had the same zeal to win. But a mountain lake has unpredictable winds that can shift very quickly and situations can become dangerous in an instant. Boats flip over, masts snap and storms can come out of nowhere.

In those days, husbands and wives often raced together—which

wasn't always the best thing as sailboat racing sometimes resulted in screaming matches. Most of the time the husband was the skipper and shouted orders to his wife who was crewing. The crew sits in front and shields most of the cold water from the skipper. It's not a ton of fun to spend hours being yelled at when you're soaking wet and needing to pee.

The wives would usually laugh it off but would make a point of coming up to me after they had knocked down a couple of cold beers. They warned me, "Never crew for your mate."

Point well taken. I actually did start crewing in some races but not with Donnie. I raced with Bob Kesselring, who liked me because I did exactly what he told me to and didn't argue. How could I argue? I didn't have a clue how to sail.

In my opinion, the smartest man at Ruedi was Paul Wirth—a kind gentleman who loved to sail but never with his wife. She was raising five children and had more to do than take off a leisurely day and drive two hours roundtrip from Aspen. Paul did bring one or more of his children, and they squealed while sailing and enjoyed swimming or playing on the beach. Paul's son Peter went on to become an active member and competitive sailor. He became one of our best friends.

As much as I got to enjoy and love these couples at Ruedi and around town, several of them sadly got divorced, and I always wondered if those sailing races added to the end of their marital bliss. I baby-sat for many of their kids at one time or another. Married or divorced, these folks became family to me.

Some regulars at the club were George and Carolyn Perry, Pat and Bill Comcowich, Bill and Vivian Goodnough, Gail and Art Preusch, Carl and Katie Bergman, Lefty and Billie Brinkman. Ironically, it was Lefty who had offered me the job teaching skiing. He was always at the lake sailing. He'd wink at me and tell me my job was available starting opening day of ski season.

In late August, as the summer season was gearing down, my psychologist guys I was housesitting for packed up to go home. How amazing that in only two months I had gotten to know them, cooked for them and become friends. We had a huge going-away party with lots of food, margaritas, music and weed. By the way, those "straight arrows" were initiated into our casual pot culture that summer and swore it should be legalized: It would really help their patients back home. When marijuana finally became legalized in Colorado, I thought back to those progressive professionals.

I'm sure their wives hardly recognized them as they got off the plane, with hair down to their shoulders, tanned like George Hamilton and with huge smiles across their previously serious faces.

Oh, what a summer in Aspen will do for one's soul.

California...and Back to Aspen

After the guys left and I no longer had a place to live, I decided to hitchhike to California with Brandy to visit my hippie brother Peter, who was now living in Berkeley and studying acupuncture. Reliving my some-times-insane hitchhiking experiences could be a book by itself so I won't elaborate. Suffice it to say, I survived. I didn't have a car in those days and flying was financially out of the question. I stayed with my brother enjoy-ing the shops, parks and carefree life of a liberal, hippie college town. Many days we'd go to the ocean and explore beaches and paths that led up beautiful forested hills. Brandy loved her first beach experience and spent the day in and out of the ocean.

One night we went to a party in the neighborhood, and I met some random guy who was driving to Yosemite National Park the next day. Did Brandy and I want to go? Did I want to learn how to climb? Sounded good to me—I wasn't on a schedule.

Yosemite was amazing. I loved the sheer massiveness of the moun-tains. The guy gave me some beginner climbing lessons and I had fun, but it was too intense for me. I didn't want to have to concentrate that hard. However, I enjoyed listening to groups of climbers at dinner. They had their own lingo and seemed so incredibly self-confident. I loved all the gear hanging from their backpacks—all the beautifully colored ropes and carabiners. It was a new sub-culture. I also admired the guys' well-sculpted bodies. They were different from skiers (although I'm sure many of them skied in the winters too).

I couldn't believe anyone had the skill and guts to climb El Capitan, although that particular day, several guys were attempting to do so. I was so in awe of the impressive rock faces. It was no surprise that these chal-lenging routes drew a slew of enthusiastic climbers. The energy surround-ing them was apparent to me—I could actually feel the electrical charge.

After a few days hiking and observing groups of people climbing, I became homesick for Aspen. I was invited to a casual party at a climber's bungalow and met so many interesting people from all around the world. I struck up a conversation with a super mellow guy around my age from Montana. Somehow I explained my situation that I had no money and didn't really want to hitchhike back to Aspen. After a couple of beers, he decided since he'd never been to Colorado and heard there was great climbing, he'd drive Brandy and me all the way home.

I was a bit worried that he'd want something in return, but realized he was a true gentleman. We spent a couple of days driving back, camping along the way. He had been so nice to me that when we arrived back in Aspen, I found a friend who loved to climb and asked if he could spend a couple of nights at his place. They climbed together up Independence Pass. I toured him around Aspen, cooked him a great dinner and he left the next day. No strings attached! Looking back, I did have a lot of luck on my side, but not always.

I crashed with Giz for a couple of nights. Once again, I had no job and no place to live. Brandy and I were walking down Hyman Avenue and Donnie passed in his Jeep with his sister Bev. They had just driven back to Aspen after having visited their parents in the Midwest. Donnie mentioned he had heard the Preuschs were looking for someone to take reservations at the Norway Lodge.

The next morning, I walked up the steep street to the large, white Norway Lodge which was above and across from the Skier's Chalet. It was a typical European-style ski and summer lodge with 16 guest rooms. It had Old-World charm that appealed to me.

I met Gail and Art Preusch and was hired. The job came with a room. They allowed Brandy to stay with me, so it was ideal. Gail and Art were incredibly kind and I became part of their family. They had two kids, Stephanie and Chris. My job was to reserve rooms the old-fashioned way—putting different colored tape onto a large poster board so you could visually see what dates were still available.

This easy job suited me well as I was allowed to go out to their pool and answer the phone. I could easily spot when people were checking in.

I'd give them the tour, advise them where to eat out, what to do and then I'd head back to the pool. Sometimes I'd look after Chris who was in middle school and a very cool kid. It was also my job to not tell what Stephanie was up to. She was in high school and very independent and a bit wild.

One day, I looked out on Aspen Street, and there was a herd of bleating sheep walking side-by-side covering the width of the street. I blinked several times thinking I was dreaming but, no, they were real. Just one more thing that astounded me about living in this magical town.

More times than not, Donnie stopped by with his beautiful Irish setter, Killy, two huskies (belonging to Al Cluck), and a black Lab named Donkey Devil. He'd honk and Brandy would dart over and jump into the Jeep for a day of fun. It warmed my heart to see my sweet dog have what is now called a play date. I was still pretty naïve, and finally it occurred to me Donnie was courting me (and Brandy, or maybe through Brandy). We were such good buddies all summer and it was so nice after Mike not to have any drama. I had lots of guy friends that I hung out with. Donnie did seem persistent, but I wasn't picking up on the signals.

In the fall, Donnie and the dogs and I went on a weekend camping trip and came back to Aspen no longer just buddies. It all sort of moved quickly after that. Donnie, Bev and I decided to live together for the winter. I had already vacated my room at the Norway Lodge for winter guests. Donnie and Bev had been living at The Glory Hole lodge but they also needed to give up their room by November. The search was on.

In those days, even though dogs roamed the streets freely (that was quickly coming to an end) it was really hard to find places to rent that allowed dogs.

Lenado

One gorgeous fall day I borrowed Donnie's Jeep and drove the eight-and-a-half miles up the Woody Creek Road (I've always called it the Lenado Road) past where the Woody Creek Tavern now resides to the logging town of Lenado to visit a college buddy who had lived up there in a tiny cabin all summer. I immediately fell in love with the area. Lenado has quite the history. In the late 1800s, the population was an amazing 300 people—they mined lead and zinc. The price of zinc climbed high and Lenado (the name means "wooded") was a hoppin' spot while that commodity was in demand. It even had a post office. Aspen local Tony Vagneur remembers that his aunts taught school there in the '30s and '40s. Everyone moved out when the price of zinc declined but in the 1960s the town was resurrected into a community of loggers. The main "drag" consisted of tiny shacks and was called "Desolation Row." As I walked around the town, I felt I was in the TV show, *Gunsmoke*. If there had been a saloon, I would have expected Matt Dillon to walk out.

I told my college buddy about our housing dilemma and he suggested I speak with Jack Flogaus, who ran the mill and rented out cabins at the time. Luckily I met Jack that day and he showed me the only available, very small one-room, unfurnished cabin. I enthusiastically put 20 dollars down for a deposit. It was mountain funky. It was very old. I figured we could all come up on weekends and hang out and cross-country ski. It was so beautiful up there. I couldn't wait to tell Donnie.

Weeks passed and there was no place available to rent so Donnie, Bev and I came up to Lenado to check out my little find. They paced around, the dogs played with sticks and, within an hour, the future was decided. We could add two crawl-in bedrooms fairly easily and insulate the place. Did I mention that Donnie's high school friend was coming out in December and would be living with us? Great, that would make our

rent affordable at five dollars a person per month.

In 1971, Lenado was a working sawmill. It's hard to believe nowadays when we drive up there for picnics that Lenado was a bustling enclave— so near Aspen yet so far from its ski culture. It was like stepping back in time. Almost all the people who lived up there worked in the mill. Well, all except us.

Everyone knows that Ashcroft, nearly thirteen miles up Castle Creek road from Aspen, was once a mining town in the 1880s with five hundred souls living and working there, but most folks overlook Lenado—she must be the jealous, forgotten sister.

The next weekend, we coaxed several friends to come up and help us build the structure with the promise of lots of food to eat and endless cold beer. We added two bedrooms side by side and cut small entrances through the wall but you had to duck down (or crawl) to get in. The bedrooms had room enough for a double mattress to go on the floor and one dresser. The decor of the main room consisted of a mattress against the far wall covered with a paisley bedspread which became our "couch." We added a few mismatched chairs later to sit in front of the stove. That was it. We didn't even have a table—bare bones and just perfect.

The guys were so high on beer that weekend they put the two-by-fours in the wrong way but it all worked out fine and the walls didn't cave in on us that winter.

No kitchen, no running water and only enough electricity to power up our car's eight-track tape player. At least we had music. We stocked up on candles and flashlights. The cabin came with an outdoor outhouse—no extra charge.

The outhouse was just a wooden structure and very drab. So, one day I put up curtains by the tiny window, hung an antique mirror and nailed in a spongy black and white toilet seat with drawings of naked women I had bought at a garage sale for a buck. I added a thick rug to warm our freezing feet and placed vases of fake colorful flowers on the wooden ledge. Martha Stewart couldn't have decorated it any better.

The first day I was at the cabin alone, a really old man with hardly any teeth, wearing a dirty, tattered plaid shirt, came up to me with a huge grin and introduced himself in a hillbilly accent. "Hi, I'm Henry and that there's Ruby." He pointed to an old lady dressed pretty much just like him collecting wood and waving at me. "We're your neighbors and I just wanted you to know how much we appreciate what you've done to our outhouse." Wait, I thought, OUR outhouse? It became immediately apparent that we shared this tiny structure that was quite far from their cabin.

I always knew I was a people-pleaser, but this sort of took it to a whole new level. Henry and Ruby fought almost every night, like two female cats. It wasn't until the end of the season we found out they were brother and sister, not a married couple. They were in their forties and not in their seventies as we had guessed. You can never judge a book by its cover. They were always nice to us and liked our dogs, so…

Bev and I spent the next couple of weeks nailing up the flat "Lenado log" siding. I will never forget the smell of that particular wood—sweet, delicious and earthy, and really intense when wet. Throughout the town there was an incredible aromatic wood smell as smoke from residents' stoves permeated the air.

Bev was quite handy so I just followed her lead, and we progressed fairly quickly until it snowed a foot one day and the work became ten times harder. We donned mukluks and built a little sled to carry the wood to our cabin. We'd haul, measure, cut and nail, again and again. It was fun and very peaceful. It's the closest I'll ever feel to being a pioneer woman. We still didn't have heat. I met a lady a few cabins away who sold us an Alaskan airtight stove for ten dollars.

Ironically, we needed wood to burn—tons of it. How funny as we now lived in the wood capital. Our neighbors thought we were crazy building in November. They all had huge, neatly stacked piles of wood around their cabins—enough for a couple of winters at least. We, however, only had scraps from our building project which would all burn in two or three nights.

For my 21st birthday, in December 1971, my parents gave me a much-needed and highly-valued chain saw. To this day, it's the best present I've ever received. As I said earlier, our neighbors worked in the mill. Why else would you live 20 miles from town with much of it being on dirt roads? It was muddy in the spring and often treacherous in the winter. Our confused neighbors never quite got used to the fact that all four of us left for work in Aspen early in the morning and didn't come back until around 10 p.m. then immediately started up the chain saw to cut wood for the night. We were way behind the eight ball.

Luckily I had met my best friend Alexia Maresi (now Haller) the summer before, and she saved me that winter by allowing me to shower at her modern apartment in town—a true luxury which made living in Lenado ideal.

Teaching Skiing

I once again need to mention Ron Anderson, aka Sherman, aka Sherm the Sperm, aka Shantz—Donnie's friend from high school in Illinois. He arrived in his huge truck in mid-December. I liked him right away—he was tall with curly, long blond hair, donned a beard and mustache and reminded me of Colonel Custer. He was the mellowest person I'd ever met. And he cracked me up all the time. He fit right into our little slice of heaven in Lenado. Looking back, I have no idea how he found our cabin that day, but he did—and immediately loved and adapted to our newly built home in the mountains.

He and Bev found two precious Siberian husky puppies from the same litter; so now we had four people and four dogs and no one ever complained about anything (well, hardly ever). Five days a week we drove into Aspen for work. Donnie and Shantz (I never called him Ron) worked at the Buttermilk Rental Shop with Jim Fox (Foxy) and a hilarious group of guys who spent all day helping tourists trying to fit into ski boots and find the correct length of skis. They kept each other laughing all day telling outrageous jokes and pulling pranks on the poor tourists to break the monotony of their workday. Donnie would come back to our cabin and relay stories about the crazy number of tourists who put their boots on the wrong feet and complained how uncomfortable they were, or the ones who actually tried to get into their bindings backwards. At least it made the day go by quickly.

Shantz had a propensity to invent things. He'd sit around after work, knock down a beer or smoke a joint, get relaxed and start relaying items he conjured up and could retire on: rose-colored goggles for skiing, toothpaste installed in a toothbrush for backpacking, zipper protectors so hippie guys who wore no undies didn't rip their penises with the sharp zipper, and many more. Ironically many of his inventions came to be patented—just not by him. To give Shantz some credit here, he later became a successful businessman.

I began my newly coveted job as ski instructor at Highlands for Lefty Brinkman. Thanksgiving arrived and I was given a ski pass, a uniform and a nametag. I took a five-day clinic to learn the GLM method of skiing. GLM stood for the "graduated length method" and was created by ski pioneer Clif Taylor.

Taylor was a Vermont native and served in the prestigious 10th Mountain Division in 1943 along with so many courageous mountain men. He and 1,200 other ski troops, trained at Camp Hale near Leadville, scaled the treacherous cliffs of Riva Ridge in Italy at night to score their biggest victory against Hitler's army. These men came home heroes, and many went on to start the famous ski areas around the country—including Aspen.

On a personal note: I'm very involved with Aspen Sister Cities. Donnie and I (along with others from the Aspen committee) traveled to Abetone, Italy, several years ago to sign a formal treaty to become Sister Cities and promote world peace. Upon meeting their mayor, I was surprised when he got misty-eyed and thanked us for the efforts of the 10th Mountain Division in saving their tiny town from annihilation by the Germans. In Aspen we have a tribute statue honoring the 10th Mountain Division in Gondola Plaza.

Our own ski clothing legend Klaus Obermeyer met Taylor in the mid-'40s in Aspen. Obermeyer says of Taylor, "He had a vision and his vision was to make it easier to learn how to ski. He taught them to dance down the mountain and not fight down the mountain."

After the war, Taylor's idea was to start students out on short skis and, as they developed the proper skills, to gradually increase the length over a week's time. It was a good concept, especially for beginners who were intimidated by strapping on very long skis. I'm not sure how long the method lasted, but ironically, years later, everyone went from their tall boards to shorter and wider versions. I remember in the '70s when Aspenites wore shirts and had bumper stickers that said "Short Skis Suck." We skiing-loving kids stuck together and thought we were the cool

THE ASPEN TIMES

Vol. 94 * No. 48 * November 27, 1975 * Aspen, Colorado 81611 * 20 Cents * 3 Sections

Up, up, and away!

On $8 a day!

This morning, Marty Tocci and Dick Prossky, both owners of $200 "Host" passes, were among the very first to board the Little Nell lift and head up into the clouds and the fresh powder snow.

Skies were gray at 9 AM when the lift started running, but first skiers down from the mountain said there were 18 inches of unbroken powder on the Back of Bell.

Chris Cassatt photo.

ones. Only tourists skied short skis back then, and we laughed behind their backs at their skis, their chic clothing and their sometimes-demanding attitudes.

53

No one wanted to wait on the Brits or anyone from New Zealand or Australia because we all knew they didn't tip in those days, and we relied on tips to survive. We especially disliked Texans because they were loud and had that accent that seemed to make their demands more obnoxious than anyone else's. Then, we all got older and wiser and realized tourists were our bread and butter.

As I matured, and sometimes hung out with Texans, I dropped my attitude and realized so many were fun-loving, kind and generous folks. And of course we all started skiing on shorter shaped skis, but continued to remain the "cool" ones!

I learned more in those five days in the ski clinic than I had the entire year before as I never had money for ski lessons. I had the best week ever. We skied hard and the seasoned instructors were patient and shared their knowledge. These instructors were older and treated me like a little sister. I was grateful that they allowed me into their circle.

After the clinic concluded, I was in charge of teaching kids and when the instructors were really busy, I would teach adults. I loved the kids— they were fearless and didn't need GLM. The adults, on the other hand, were anxious and always had differing opinions on what slopes to ski and what time to take breaks and eat lunch. I was way too young and imma-ture to take the upper hand. I realized right away I was the low gal on the totem pole. They gave me the "never-nevers," which meant I had total beginners. They were typically 30- to 40-year-old women whose hus-bands or boyfriends wanted them to learn how to ski and were smart enough not to teach them. So I got them.

I had envisioned getting a group of cool kids I could take down blue runs as I had seen tons of instructors do. I guess you have to start some-where. I used more of my college *Intro to Psychology* pointers than my newly acquired ski skills.

The never-nevers and I stayed on the short chairlift at the bottom of the mountain. We'd take the lift up, they'd fall down, I'd help them up and they'd fall down again. And so it went. Luckily we took lots of breaks, and some of the ladies were sore and bruised and left after lunch. I was really kind and patient so I was tipped well and even got some great invitations to have dinner in town with them, a luxury I couldn't afford on my own.

However, I was restless. I had only one day off to free ski. January arrived, and with it a dwindling numbers of tourists. I often showed up to teach and there weren't enough people signed up for classes. No teaching, no money. But alas, they were looking for someone to help Bayless, the nice guy I had befriended at the short beginner chair lift. He needed someone to punch lift tickets.

NEWS FLASH for you millennials: in those days you wore a lift ticket attached to your jacket or gloves and a person had to punch that ticket—there were no computer scanners.

I did that job for the slow month of January. Aspen got busy again in February so for an entire week, I went back to teaching never-nevers.

Most weekends, friends came up to our cabin in Lenado for cross-country ski adventures up Larkspur Mountain. There are endless trails to explore. We'd come back home exhausted and since all we could really cook was boiling water, we lived on "just add water" meals. With a loaf of French bread from the Mesa Store Bakery on Main Street and some marijuana brownies, what could be better? We'd laugh well into the night, tell jokes and ski stories and quite often, our friends would pass out contently on our mattress (which also served as a couch) on the floor in the main room.

By then, we had figured out adding coal to the fire meant we didn't have to draw straws to see which poor fool had to get up at four in the morning to add wood to the burned-out stove. Nights were cozy and warm.

One weekend, after a fun time with friends, I sat down by the stove with Donnie and had a long talk. I was honest and told him I knew it was a huge honor to have been asked by Lefty to teach skiing. But I realized I had little patience and what I really wanted to do was to ski. He encouraged me to quit with one of his all-time famous lines, "The things you worry about the most turn out for the best."

The next day, I approached Lefty with sweaty palms and a pain in my gut and explained my dilemma—profusely apologizing and rambling on and on about how grateful I was for the opportunity he had given me.

He put up his hand to shut me up, looked me in the eye and said, "I never do a job I don't enjoy at least 90 percent." I almost cried with relief. In the next breath he explained that the gal who booked private lessons had to go home to help her ill mother. Did I want her job?

It was available five days a week from 7:45 to 10 a.m. I could ski the rest of the day and then be back from 3 to 5 p.m. I'd do his dreaded paperwork on slow days. I couldn't believe my luck. The rest of the season was better than I could have imagined.

Lefty was in the office while I booked private lessons. He was self-assured, funny, charismatic and endlessly flirted with the women. He poured his charm onto anyone who'd listen. He told constant one-liner jokes. He was an accomplished ice-skater, skier, tennis player, sailor—an all-around athlete. Everyone who worked at Highlands had a Lefty story. He eventually moved from Aspen and managed a guest ranch in Wickenburg, Arizona, as well as the Lake Placid Club in New York. Surprisingly he passed away prematurely, but remains one of Aspen's characters.

Once in awhile I taught skiing when they really needed me, but most days I free-skied to my heart's content, often with the ski patrolmen or with other ski instructors on their days off. Everyone was extremely friendly and we formed a little Highlands family. I was improving by the day and I'm pretty sure I skied with a smile across my face. I could have been the entrepreneur who invented the slogan, "Life Is Good." I would have sewn it on every piece of clothing I owned.

Last Dance in Lenado

Sadly, winter ended. Lenado was no longer a lovely, snow-covered town smelling of delicious wood smoke. The snow was melting and spring in Lenado meant mud—thick, messy mud. Our dogs were clean only when they slept inside. Otherwise, they were filthy.

Bev, Shantz, Donnie and I sat down one spring evening and discussed the future. We hatched a plan to live in town. I got a hot tip from a ski instructor friend that a two-bedroom unit was available at the Agate lodge on Seventh Street, around the corner from the Forest Service. I still didn't own a car and Lenado, as much as we loved it, seemed 100 miles farther away in the springtime. We were torn.

We finally checked out the Agate and declared it perfect for the four of us, plus they allowed our dogs. Granted, the rent was no longer 20 dollars. But at 100 dollars, we figured we could swing it somehow. The Agate was an old building and in the 1950s had a gas station attached to one side. We loved the huge picture windows and the red wood carved aspen leaves on the outside walls.

The first thing we saw was a large kitchen with running water, an enormous living room with a huge fireplace, two bathrooms and a bedroom that was bigger than the main room in our Lenado cabin. We never found the second bedroom but we figured that we could build a loft for Bev and Shantz off the main room and everyone would live like royalty. We could walk or cycle to town. We'd be able to move in late May, which gave us a little more time in Lenado.

It was going to be really sad to leave our mountain cabin where the dogs ran to their hearts' content. We had loved our winter roughing-it experience beyond words. We had learned a lot—like how not to put the two-by-fours in backwards and how to operate a chain saw. I'd miss the smells of wood fires wafting through the town; the challenge of driving

57

home in the late evenings on often icy, dark roads; neighbors we hardly knew randomly dropping by cookies or inviting us "young folks" to dinner; and yes, even the shared outhouse. Our cabin was situated down by the roaring creek and the sound of rushing water put us to sleep nightly. In the spring, the sound of rain pouring on our roof was deafening at first and then rhythmic. The earthy spring smells were strong, yet aromatic.

We told Jack we'd be vacating our cabin the end of May so he had time to find someone to rent it. He was pleased with all the work we had done and planned on doubling the rent! We cherished and dreaded the remaining warm, mud-filled days. We had a little potluck going-away party before we left and enjoyed getting to know some of the neighbors we hadn't yet met. We had become so elusive in the winter season; we never really spent much time with these amazing folks. The good news, they told us, was that we could come back to visit them anytime we wanted.

I never told anyone until now, but the last day in our cabin, I borrowed Donnie's Swiss Army knife and carved our names into the wood on the side facing the creek. For posterity. To remember that we had lived in this special place for even a short while. To leave our mark.

We left our mattresses, airtight stove and newly decorated outhouse to whomever moved in next. Years later, I was on Ambergris Caye, an island off Belize, when some children found out I was an author and asked if I would visit their little island school. These lovely children attended school in several pastel-painted cottages right on the beach, on prime ocean-front property. In a palapa, with exotic sea breezes blowing, I shared with them the process of writing a book. As small world stories go, I met the headmistress, Dixie Bowen, and we traced back that it was she who moved into our cabin that spring. And here, forty years later, we meet on a faraway island in the Caribbean. That's Aspen for ya!

It was Dixie who told me about the Lenado reunion that next summer. She flew in for it. Frank and Margie Peters, who still own a cabin there, hosted the party in a meadow above the town, and I chatted with old acquaintances and people I had never met before. I loved hearing all the stories and it brought me back to the winter of 1971 as if I'd never left.

During our time in Lenado, it was a good thing we didn't have Facetime, Instagram, Internet or digital cameras to upload photos back then. If our parents had seen our living conditions, they would have croaked! Years later when my parents came out to visit, I drove them up the windy dirt road to the ghost town of Lenado. The mill had closed in 1975 and most folks had moved elsewhere. My parents stared in disbelief and then howled—they thought it was the most hilarious thing in the world. My dad, a hobby photographer took tons of photos so my mom, a professional artist, could paint the quaint mountain town and cabins for her Old West series. What great stories they had for their friends back home.

The Agate Lodge

I spent Saturdays going to garage sales to shop for now-needed kitchen items and furniture. By June, we were ready to move. It took us one Jeep and one truckload to move our belongings. We laughed endlessly—it was like moving into a mansion. We couldn't begin to fill all the empty spaces.

I found great deals on hanging plants—people were moving out of town and practically giving them away. Thus began my obsession with making macramé hangings to secure our long, hanging plants. I so admired the numerous plants in the ever-popular restaurant, Andre's, and tried to duplicate them. What I remember most about Andre's restaurant on Galena Street was the welcoming feeling when you first walked in. Hanging plants of all shapes and sizes were unique in Aspen at the time and gave off a nice energy. The wooden Victorian tables added to the ambiance and the food was outstanding. I still remember their omelettes and mouth-watering French toast. The pretty waitresses were friendly and happy to be there.

The Agate was like moving into a commune. It covered an entire block. On Hallam Street, there were funky little cabins. A large building faced Seventh Street consisted of our roomy apartment, a one-room apartment attached to our east wall and several apartments on the opposite side facing the alley. Across the alley was a large house where Jughead and Nancy Bogle Brown lived. It was summer so we were outside every opportunity we had.

The best part was a large common grassy yard where everyone converged in the late afternoons for drinks and food. The people I remember were Sue Serry, Will and Mark Ferry, Sandy and Sue, Charlie Starr, Nancy Lovendahl and Scott Keating, Jimmy C. and Teri, Tim Cooney, Steve and Donna and many more. Everyone was fun and interesting and loved to talk! We would barbecue and socialize for hours. We didn't need to spend

money at a bar—all our new friends surrounded us, free of charge. After all these years, I often run into my neighbors from the Agate who still live in Aspen, and we reminisce about those special times we had—they were more relaxed and free.

Being in town we no longer had to get up in the dark, come home after dark, chop wood and make a fire, use an outhouse and drive those scary roads. Here, we had so many more opportunities to be social and discover more what town had to offer.

Brandy was in heaven. We inherited a tether ball game. Brandy could

wind that ball around the pole in one direction, watch it unwind and then wind it the opposite direction—all with just her nose. She was a pro and entertained us all for hours.

When we lived at the Agate we didn't have a TV. One of our favorite sources of entertainment was during winter snowstorms. We'd make a roaring fire, plop up our feet, a cocktail in hand, and wait for cars to drive too fast around the corner. The Agate was on the straight section of Seventh Street before it takes a sharp left onto Hallam, which leads out of town. I can't tell you how hilarious it was to see car after car skid on the icy road. You'd think these drivers would figure out to slow down, but they didn't. Some cars lost control and wound up over the curb and on the Forest Service yard. Stuck. We only went outdoors to assist if we felt anyone actually got hurt (this was rare). This doesn't seem to happen anymore as the snow plows do a great job, but in the '70s, drivers who drove too fast during snowstorms often suffered the consequences.

Donnie was teaching sailing for the City of Aspen Recreation Department and told me about an opening to run a hiking program. I had an interview with the intimidating Teddy Armstrong, Donnie's boss. He was a very large (fat) man and constantly yelled at his employees. He scared the living daylights out of me. He was looking to hire someone to lead hikes for kids. I couldn't believe this offer: another chance to get paid to do something fun. I got the job.

AGATE BROWNIES

½ cup melted butter (then cooled)

¼ cup milk

3 eggs

1¼ cups flour

⅔ cup of a good quality cocoa powder

2 cups sugar

½ tsp baking powder

Pinch salt

Preheat oven to 350 degrees.

Mix the dry ingredients together in one bowl.

In another bowl, whisk the eggs and milk, then add the cooled butter.

Add the wet ingredients into the dry ingredients and mix thoroughly with a spatula. Do not over mix.

Use a 7½ inch x 11 inch glass pan lined with either foil or parchment paper. Bake for 30 minutes or until a toothpick comes out clean.

Sift powdered sugar before serving. Serve with ice cream or whipped cream.

More Lessons to Learn

Every Tuesday and Thursday I'd meet kids in Paepcke Park, pack them in the City van, drive somewhere and hike for the day. We never hiked the same trail twice. We hiked the Weller Lake Trail, the Braille Trail, Crater Lake above the Maroon Bells, and Hanging Lake down near Glenwood Springs. The kids were mostly out-of-towners along with some locals. They were so much fun as they had no expectations and were happy to be outdoors.

A month into the season, I expanded the program with Teddy's consent to overnight camping trips. I learned two very valuable lessons on our first overnight. First, check out the hike before assuming 10-year-old kids would think it's easy, and second, always do a pack check. Bev, Shantz and I were the hiking chaperones for eight kids under the age of

eleven. They showed up on time with their backpacks. All I asked in preparation was that they had water, snacks and a sleeping bag. I wasn't specific beyond that.

I made the mistake of not going through each pack to see what Mom or Dad had stuffed in. I also didn't check to make sure their packs fit them. Of all places to go, I randomly chose American Lake up Castle Creek before Ashcroft. It's three miles uphill with steep switchbacks. The hike was harder carrying a heavy pack. Bev, Shantz and I carried all the food, cook gear, stove and tents. My pack felt as if it weighed 100 pounds after just 20 minutes of hiking. The kids started groaning immediately.

We checked their packs and couldn't believe what the parents had packed for their kids. Some had packed enough for a weeklong trip to Disneyland complete with their "blankie" and favorite stuffed animal. Okay, I realized I was the stupid one. How could I have expected these city parents to know what to bring and what not to? Three boys were from the same family from Los Angeles and their dad had packed a blow-up canoe. Really?

Shantz was sweet and took a load of unnecessary items back to the van. One poor kid had his dad's backpack, which was way too big for him, so I gave him my smaller one and wore his. We evenly distributed items until all the kids were happy again and raring to go.

It was a gorgeous day, the sun was hot and everyone had sweat pouring off of them. We told jokes and sang songs and very slowly made our way to the lake. When we finally arrived, we all discarded our packs and jumped into the lake to cool off. We set up camp, fished, made dinner and sat around the campfire while Shantz mesmerized the kids with scary ghost stories under a starlit sky. We all slept like the dead. We got up in the morning, cooked breakfast, packed up and headed down the trail.

It was easier going downhill and our packs were much lighter. The kids practically ran down. We were a bit late arriving at the park. The kids were so enthusiastic telling their parents how much fun it was and could they go again in a couple of days? The dad from L.A. with the three boys tipped us 100 dollars, which was a fortune in 1972.

Teddy yelled at me because I was late returning the van. I was too excited about this first successful overnight that I really didn't care. I got used to Teddy growling like a bear but realized he was a softie under all that skin.

Shantz and I took out several more overnights that summer but after that first trip, we learned to simply drive somewhere with all the gear and kids. We'd set up base camp and would hike from there with just a small daypack filled with water and snacks. The kids were happier, and Shantz and I loved the newly created stress-free trips. And Teddy was thrilled the van was back when I predicted.

The summer season ended and most of the tourists left the last week in August and Aspen became quiet again. Kids went back to school, the streets were empty except on long weekends when tourists drove to Aspen to view the gorgeous fall foliage. All was well in my world and I was excited that ski season was right around the corner.

Barbara Guy—a Mostly True Story

As I was writing these vignettes I attended the 50th anniversary for the Aspen Yacht Club. Peter Wirth came from as far as Grand Junction and many other old-timers showed up. I sat at one of the wooden picnic tables right outside the newly spruced-up shack of yesteryear and ate dinner with Peter and Barbara Guy. I realized then and there I needed to include something about Barbara.

Everyone knows Barbara but, in case you're not from Aspen or are too young, I'll do my best to describe this bigger-than-life, fun-loving, longtime local (however, she and Peter moved to New Castle years ago). Barbara has one of the best laughs of anyone I know. She's short, but tall in kindness and heart. I've never seen Barbara with long hair, and for some reason, she's so animated that her face easily turns red. She's never been skinny and, as far as I know, she's never dieted yet looks fantastically healthy.

I first met Barbara at the Yacht Club back in the '70s. Donnie decided, after heavy persuading from Barbara, to add a two-day adults learn-to-sail class. Donnie would teach them the basics in town at the Hotel Jerome pool, give them a swim test, teach the various knots and show them (using a toy sailboat) how the winds work to "come about" and "jibe" and the different points of sailing.

Barbara, Hjordis Skaeringsson, Sigrid Stapleton and Helen Gloor showed up at the Yacht Club ready to go with bathing suits, towels, sun-tan lotion, water, wine (of course), a change of clothing and huge coolers filled with amazing food for lunch as well as potluck items for a picnic in the late afternoon.

I didn't arrive until later as I had to work but didn't want to miss out on the potluck. These ladies were older than I. They had families and kid obligations, and they loved to cook. Barbara and Peter owned the Steak

Pit restaurant, and she made the delicious soups as well as her famous hot fudge which melted over their popular hot-fudge sundaes.

Sigrid Stapleton was married to David whose great grandparents came to Aspen in 1881 in a covered wagon from Leadville over Taylor Pass—true story. She had a large family with five wonderful children and cooked all the time. (During the process of writing this chapter, Sigrid sadly passed away.)

Hjordis was married to Ulfar and they migrated to Aspen from Reykjavik, Iceland, the winter of 1960. Hjordis taught skiing at Buttermilk and was referred to as "Queen Bee." She was well known for her festive holiday feasts, but I vividly remember her lying by the Glory Hole pool with Marian Lunow in the hot sun getting super tanned and drinking wine early in the day. They lay there day after day in their skimpy strapless swimsuits chatting and laughing for hours. Helen was married to Fred Gloor, who loved to sail and wanted Helen to feel more comfortable crewing.

Donnie told me that from the moment the ladies arrived, he knew it was going to be a wild day. He had borrowed mismatched adult life jackets and the first hour was spent with the ladies haggling over who got which colorful life jacket and trying to figure out how to squeeze their large chests inside and somehow getting them zipped up.

They were so exhausted after this strenuous task they opened a bottle of white wine to ease the anxiety of having to actually sail. The one thing they hadn't practiced at the Hotel Jerome pool was what to do when the boat capsized. Donnie did a demonstration in the cove and the ladies clapped with glee at how fun it looked.

He showed them how to rig the Sunfish sailboats and, with total confidence and another swig of wine, off they went two to a boat. The cove at the Yacht Club is narrow so it involves several tacking maneuvers to get out on the lake. Each boat started off surprisingly well. Donnie was in the motor rescue boat and was impressed—most beginners crash into the banks of the cove. But the ladies actually tacked in plenty of time and ducked their heads as the boom came across. He was thinking—this is a piece of cake. I can sit back and get a nice tan.

But just when they got out of the cove, the crazy, wild, shifty winds

of Ruedi kicked in. Donnie was yelling at the ladies to do this and that but they were laughing and not paying any attention. First one boat flipped on its side and then the next one flipped. Instead of quickly jumping onto the daggerboard to get the boat right side up (like the kids do), the ladies started swimming around the boat thinking this was a lovely way to spend the afternoon.

Meanwhile, Donnie threw an anchor off the side of the motorboat and jumped in. He got one boat up but Barbara and Sigrid were over with Hjordis and Helen splashing water and thinking this was a pool party.

Donnie sailed over and had Barbara and Sigrid get in. He lowered their sail. He had to swim a long way to the other boat, which had drifted. He righted that boat and somehow hoisted Hjordis and Helen up by their bathing suit bottoms and told them to stay put. He lowered their sail. Hjordis was thrilled because she had smuggled her bottle of wine onto the boat and stuck it in a cubby and it was still there even though the glasses were not.

As they were passing the bottle around, Donnie now had to swim back to get his motorboat. The winds were howling and white caps had formed. Rather than repeating this scenario he simply threw the ladies a line and slowly towed them back to shore. Once again the ladies were ecstatic—a day away from chores, kids and cooking.

They helped Donnie roll up the sails, put away the daggerboards and immediately laid their towels on the beach. They spread out an array of delicious snacks with yet another bottle of wine and got down to the serious business of sun-bathing.

About that time I was driving down the twisty dirt road to the Yacht Club in my beloved '48 Willys Jeep, Harvey and I could hear the ladies laughing all the way down the hill. By now, it was late afternoon. Donnie took the ladies and me out for a motorboat ride around Ruedi. The howling winds had died down and it was calm as glass. The ladies were in rare form telling jokes and tall tales.

After a day on the water with sun and wind, everyone was quite ravenous. When we got back to the beach, the ladies started taking salads and fried chicken out of their coolers for dinner. It was a feast.

In those days, many people owned an ice-cream maker—it was a fad. Some were electric and some were the old-fashioned hand-cranking kind. Both Sigrid and Barbara had made ice cream for the "party," and Sigrid announced that her vanilla ice cream was the best ever which prompted Barbara to disagree that, no, hers was the most delicious. Ever-calm Donnie said he couldn't wait to do a taste test.

Barbara and Sigrid confidently dished out their creations. Not to hurt anyone's feelings, Donnie and I said both were beyond delicious. That was not the answer the ladies were looking for—they expected a winner. The next thing we knew, the ladies ran onto the beach with their buckets of ice cream and started throwing handfuls at each other. Donnie and I sat back laughing in disbelief, watching these grown women let loose.

Donnie got smart. The next day, he took each lady out on the Sunfish and taught them all he possibly could. I'm not sure they ever learned to sail but there were plenty of empty wine bottles in the trash and loads of good food consumed.

Donnie never taught an adult sailing class again.

BARBARA GUY'S PEPPERMINT ICE CREAM
WITH DARK CHOCOLATE SAUCE

1 lb peppermint stick
  candy
1 pint (2 cups) milk
1 pint (2 cups) heavy
  cream
1 bar (4 oz) Baker's
  German sweet
  chocolate

5 T water
¼ cup sugar
Dash salt
1 T Butter
¼ tsp vanilla

Soak the candy overnight in the milk. Whip the cream
and add this before freezing. The candy sweetens,
flavors and colors the cream pink! Barbara uses an old
wooden tub ice cream freezer (electric), but any ice
cream machine works fine. Freeze according to your
machine's directions.

Freeze to the consistency that you like, remove the
paddle and place in your freezer until ready to serve.

For the sauce: combine the chocolate, water, sugar and
salt in a saucepan. Cook and stir over low heat until the
ingredients are blended and the sauce is smooth.
Remove from the heat and stir in the butter and vanilla.
Serve warm or chilled over the ice cream.

*This is a Guy family favorite. It has a wonderful texture and a
beautiful color. Sometimes Barbara is lucky enough to find
giant candy canes. This makes unwrapping the small, round
peppermint candies a little easier.*

Oops

Fall in Aspen arrived and we said goodbye to the hundreds of tourists seeking a mountain vacation. Even though I loved skiing, when the aspen trees turned their brilliant yellows and oranges, we took to hiking all the mountain trails. We always looked forward to our annual hike over East Maroon pass to the smaller and more laid-back town of Crested Butte.

Fall was also a time to prepare for the long winter ahead. The Stihl chain saw I got for my birthday was a great asset. Sandy Lunow who ran The Glory Hole lodge hired Donnie, Shantz and me to cut wood for their fireplaces. Besides paying us a decent fee, he promised us a free dinner at the restaurant attached to the lodge, the Captain's Anchorage. We rarely ate dinner out back then, so we were ecstatic.

We'd get up early, have a big breakfast at the Village Pantry, drink enough coffee to cut down a forest, slab on baby oil with iodine (I can still remember that smell) and drive way past the town of Lenado to the upper logging roads.

Donnie had some experience cutting tall trees as he had worked summers in high school at a camp and had worked on a Forest Service crew for a week. He said it was a "piece of cake." We worked well as a team and felt strong like true lumberjacks. The guys would saw the bottom of a dead tree and when it was time, they'd yell, "timber," and then we'd all go running so as not to be crushed. We worked hard and were focused. Covered with sweat and rubbing sore arms, we allowed ourselves a couple of breaks. When the truck was filled as high as possible, we'd tie the logs down and head down the mountain.

It was hard work, but fun and rewarding. As I mentioned earlier, Shantz was truly one of the funniest guys I'd ever met. He'd just look at me and I'd laugh for no reason. Plus, he'd take on a Southern accent that cracked me up since he's from Illinois. No wonder Donnie loved his high school buddy.

We stopped in "town" to visit our Lenado friends before driving
back to Aspen. We'd arrive at The Glory Hole lodge, put on our leather
gloves, drop off the heavy logs and begin the arduous task of cutting
each log into small pieces that would fit into the fireplaces. We also had
to cut tons of kindling. Then we'd stack the wood into neat piles and
clean up all the mess we'd made.

Exhausted, we'd drive back to the Agate, craving a "cold one." I'm
not a beer drinker but after a woodcutting day, a few sips of the ice-cold
liquid were heavenly. This job for the Glory Hole took us two full weeks.
The last day, we were all excited and way too lax and weren't paying
attention. Donnie felled a tree—yep—right into the truck. It smashed
the entire back window. Holy crap! We couldn't believe our eyes.

We weren't exactly insured for this kind of freak accident, so we all
chipped in our hard-earned cash to fix the damn window. Life is all about
learning lessons, right? At least we had had fun, got great tans, grew
fabulous biceps and still made a little extra money. We thoroughly
enjoyed our dinner at the Anchorage and had a great story to tell for
many years after.

Gretl's

I was up at the Ruedi Reservoir in the late fall to help Donnie put away all the City boats and gear. Lefty was there and came up to me to explain that the lady who worked the private-lesson desk had come back to town after helping out her mom the winter before. I would no longer have that job unless I wanted it on her one day off. I could still teach. We drove back to Aspen and I faced the reality that I didn't have a job. I had decided teaching skiing was not my thing.

But, per usual, within a few days I heard that Gretl Uhl, who ran the famous, quaint little restaurant at the base of Tourtelotte Park on Aspen Mountain, was looking for someone part-time during the lunch rush in exchange for a full ski pass. I went to her little Victorian house in the West End, sat down at her kitchen table covered with a Bavarian tablecloth and was served piping hot delicious apple strudel and strong, black coffee. We chatted for hours. It was the best interview I ever had.

Gretl moved to Aspen in 1953 and fulfilled her dream of owning an authentic European-style restaurant in the mountains. Her family owned and operated such a restaurant in Garmisch-Partenkirchen, Germany (our first Sister City). Gretl couldn't believe skiers were happy with canned soups and packaged foods. She wanted to serve skiers the best food, everything fresh and homemade. It didn't take long for skiers to realize where to eat on Aspen Mountain.

She developed her own recipe for apple strudel and it was a phenomenon. This delicious dessert was highly coveted. People loved it, they stood in long lines for it, they dreamt about it and they reserved it like a limited fine wine. Devotees from all around the country ordered it so they could savor it at home. This concoction of homemade pastry, wrapped around apples (peeled and cored by an antique hand-operated machine) had customers drooling. Many customers were truly addicted.

I was hired on the spot. Gretl relayed my job description: I would carefully and delicately cut the famous strudel and hide it for skiers who had reserved it. I'd add homemade whipped cream and later I'd call out grill orders. Sounded great to me. Plus, I could eat whatever was left in the strudel pan—well, everyone on the line split what was left. I would work the two-hour lunch rush, five days a week for a ski pass.

There is really nothing that compares to the smell of Gretl's freshly baked strudel. Skiers would tell me they could smell it half way up Ajax. Gretl worked hard every day of ski season. She would be up at the restaurant early, work all day and always had a smile on her face. Gretl often wore her German dirndl to work and her hair was always perfect. She looked like she was going out for a fancy luncheon instead of running a busy restaurant. She was short and didn't look athletic, but, boy, could she ski. One afternoon when I worked late, she asked me to ski down the mountain with her. Sure, but I thought I'd have to wait every few seconds. She took off and I barely saw her until we reached the bottom of Little Nell. Unbeknownst to me she had been on the German National Team and totally surprised me that day.

I loved everyone I worked with: PJ, Sigrid Stapleton, Bryce Maple, Sally Mencimer, Barbara Guy, Rob Baxter, Nina, Leslie, Gus and Carol, Captain, Chris and Julie. Many of the crew worked my opposite shift: Peter, Jimmy, Russel, David, John, Tim, Owen and Kenny. How lucky we were to have worked at Gretl's.

At the end of the day, no matter the weather conditions, Gretl would be one of the last skiers down, right before the patrol sweep. Little did anyone know, but in her backpack, she carried hundreds of dollars from the day's cash register—this was before most people used credit cards. Luckily, she always made it to the bank safely.

GRETL'S CRUMB CAKE

2 sticks butter

1 cup sugar

6 egg yolks

1 cup all-purpose flour

1 cup cake flour

2 small squares Baker's semi-sweet chocolate, grated

1 cup hazelnuts, walnuts or pecans, ground up

1 tsp baking powder

6 egg whites

2 cups heavy whipping cream

1 tsp vanilla

2 T rum (more if desired)

Confectioners' sugar

Beat the first 3 ingredients until creamy. Add the flours, the grated chocolate, then nuts and the baking powder. Beat the egg whites and fold gently into the mixture. Grease parchment paper or waxed paper and place around a 10-inch spring-form pan. Bake at 350 degrees for 50-60 minutes or until a toothpick comes out clean. Let cool.

Whip the heavy cream with a little confectioners' sugar and the vanilla until stiff.

When the cake is cooled (not warm at all) take a long knife and cut approximately 1 inch off the top of the cake, all the way around. Place that piece into a bowl (you'll be making it into crumbs so no need to be careful). Scoop approximately 2 inches out of the cake so that you leave the sides and the bottom—you'll end up with a cake shell.

Take all scooped-out cake and make into crumbs. Reserve 1 cup of these crumbs. Take the large amount of crumbs and mix with the whipped cream. Take the rum and sprinkle it over the bottom of the cake shell. Take the whipped cream and crumb mixture and fill it back into the cake shell, scatter the reserved crumbs on top and lightly sprinkle with confectioners' sugar.

Gretl says to make this cake one day, pour the rum over it and fill the second day and serve the third day. We had a recipe testing party and Gretl kindly showed us how to make it. We made it in the morning and watched Gretl fill it the evening of the same day. Of course we ate it and it was amazing—we couldn't wait another day.

Ski Gangs

I've done many sports in my life but, I have to say, skiing remains my favorite. Every time I get out there on any mountain, within the first turn, I feel the joy and freedom skiing brings me. When I first started skiing Aspen Mountain, all I ever heard about was the Bell Mountain Buck-Off (or known to many as the Rumble on the Ridge). It happened every year mid-April and gave the ski gangs a chance to strut their stuff. The first time I went I couldn't believe how many people showed up to cheer on these daring groups of expert skiers. It was an Aspen happening and the Flyers (many people know them as the Flynn Flyers), the Bell Mountain Buckaroos and the Acme Racing Team did not disappoint.

That's when the reality of ski gangs appeared in my consciousness. I loved the idea of skiing with a bunch of friends like the other ski gangs did. They pushed each other, and I was a fan. Our gang, the Powder Sluts, began when Mari Peyton, Polly Ross and Karen Kraft got together to ski on powder days, as other friends didn't enjoy skiing in blizzards when conditions could be challenging. Once I learned to ski powder, I realized skiing in a "whiteout" was a bonus since it left most people in front of a fire drinking hot chocolate or something stronger.

One eight-inch powder day at Snowmass, Mari, Karen and Polly were skiing together and a random guy got on the double chairlift with Mari and said, "I've been following you gals. You're just a bunch of powder sluts." And the term stuck. Adding to that crew was Gail Check and Michaela Game. And with time, others joined in.

A year later on an epic powder day, I ran into the ladies at Snowmass after skiing with Donnie, and they asked me to join them. I was honored and we skied many "secret" spots where we had fresh tracks hours after the tourists skied the main runs. I was one of the Powder Sluts before the day was over!

This is how it worked for us: In the early morning, if there was more than six inches of powder, we'd all get on speed dial (yes on land lines) and yell out, "powder alert." We usually met at Snowmass Mountain the second the lift started in order to get first tracks. There's a transferable energy that happens when several people are whooping and hollering and enjoying the same rush of skiing fresh, untracked powder. Of course, I love to ski by myself but something magical happens in a group.

We were not sluts and were not promiscuous but we lived for powder (and still do). Okay, if you want to know the acronym: sluts stands for "seeking light, untracked snow."

We were so proud of our ski gang that we had ski suits with our gang name embroidered on the back and hats to identify us. I always loved when four or five of us flew into a lift line laughing and excited, and someone would comment on how cool it was that we loved to ski powder so much.

Another distant memory was of the slow chairlifts. Yes, the high-speed chairs have their benefits but many of us at the time of transition were saddened that we could no longer have a long conversation or get to know someone in the time it took to get to the top. Plus, the powder snow got skied out much faster. Mari was so upset she started making up a song to the tune of "Slow Hand" by the Pointer Sisters. Other Sluts added lines.

Slow Lift
I want a mountain with a slow lift
Snow that's soft and light with deep drifts
On a long slow ride with only you by my side
What secrets we do confide
As we let our legs rest
That's when you first confessed
You like skiing with me the best

The Dick Barrymore Hot Dog Contest is officially off ... However ... A party might be held on the ridge of Bell Mountain Friday, March 10th, from 10 a.m. to 3 p.m. to celebrate Spring and have a bash. All skiers who want to may bring refreshments and cameras. If anyone desires to show off his free style ability and hot dog technique he shall be welcome. Prizes might be awarded and it is rumored that Barrymore's cameras may be operating in the vicinity.

The Fantom

THE ASPEN TIMES

Vol. No. 91 * No. 10 * Aspen, Colorado 81611 * March 9, 1972 * 15 Cents

One year, we had a decorated float in the Wintersköl parade and belted out the song, waved a lot and threw out candy to the kids.

Of course, I remember how I struggled when I first began. And I know how hard it is to learn to flow effortlessly through powder snow. I have many girlfriends who come out to visit and will only ski on bluebird days with hard-packed snow. The minute it starts to snow over four inches, they tell me suddenly they don't know how to ski anymore, and they don't like to ski in a snowstorm. As I've said before, skiing powder takes a totally new skill set. I've always loved the quiet solitude of skiing in a quiet blizzard. You see by feeling the snow and staying close to the trees for some definition.

I vividly remember the day I "got it." I had always tried to power my way through the snow. One day I simply quit fighting and the magic happened. I couldn't teach this to anyone. I'm sure every skier has had that moment at one time or another when you just feel one with the mountain. It's a very personal, spiritual feeling and it keeps you coming back over and over.

A few years back, the Historical Society had an event and invited all present and past ski gangs. We Powder Sluts showed up in full force as did so many gangs that I never knew about.

In those days we didn't have the "fat boys" or the wide skis that help to ski powder more easily. We were all strong skiers who truly had a huge passion for the fluff. We were known to take off work on a powder morning and work extra hours on the weekends. It was true—we couldn't get enough.

Later, I was fortunate to go heli-skiing in the Bugaboos in British Columbia with a different group of amazing ladies and we were called, "Chix on Stix." This was the ultimate—to wake up each morning in a mountain lodge accessed only by helicopter and to ski untracked powder all day long with Chix who made you laugh and who appreciated the fact that we were the luckiest people on earth.

The Wet T-Shirt Contest

Winter of 1972–73 arrived and Donnie landed the coveted job of ski patrolman at Snowmass Mountain. What a fun job for him. He could ski all day, go on a few rescues, and spend his time in the midst of some of the craziest, funniest and happiest guys on the planet. The ski patrol shack is a place where they could do a reality TV show. To while away the time when not out on patrol, the guys played games, told every joke ever invented and pulled pranks on each other. They took their job seriously but a lot of their time was "downtime." They were a mischievous bunch— like college boys. Can you imagine going to work and finding that overnight the guys had taken off your bindings and screwed them on backwards? Or you found mushy oatmeal in your ski boots? They became very close and often partied together after work.

Where in the world would you have the opportunity to work with guys with such fun and colorful nicknames? Donnie's nickname was Lips. Some of these guys are now in their seventies and still go by these names: Hippie Hyrup, Furry Fred, Tommy Sue, Dinky, Wall Street, Johnny Sawpit, Elk Camp Bob, Pig Pen, Suitcase Stan, Mad Dog, Shithouse/Stink-foot Sewell.

The ski patrol wives and girlfriends became friendly as well. I met them all at the various parties and some of us formed a group called "Stitch and Bitch." In fact, most of us are still here nearly five decades later and, although we don't meet once a month anymore, we do meet yearly for a cookie swap. Over the years, as a group, we made quilts for one another and created wonderful baby pillows; we went to each other's weddings and welcomed babies and grandbabies into our lives; we stitched beautiful friendships together and, yes, we bitched together. It's been an honor to be a part of these ladies' lives.

It was fun for me to be on Aspen Mountain after skiing Aspen Highlands for several winters. I learned all the trails and met new people to ski with. I treasured my "family" at Gretl's and often skied with them after my shift. I was barely paying my rent so I baby-sat many evenings. Someone at Gretl's said she was working après-ski at the Holiday Inn near Buttermilk, and they needed cocktail waitresses.

I was handed my neon orange hot pants uniform. Are you kidding me? No, they were not. The job was easy enough: I served a variety of crazy-named cocktails for two hours in (lucky for me) a dark bar. I served mostly middle-aged men who called me "Nurse." After I got over my initial shock of the uniform and occasional pinching, I rather enjoyed the tempo and the tips. Strudel cutter by day and nurse by night—I adapt well.

My only rebellion was the winter when the Holiday Inn hosted the "Wet T-Shirt Contest," an extremely popular event with no need to explain further. All the après-ski staff was expected to work this event. Every man in town attended along with some women who wanted to watch the action. I showed up with an outfit I borrowed from a friend. A blue-jean jumper with a cute red-checkered blouse underneath—very Western and yet casual. My boss asked me when I was going to change into my uniform. I knew he needed cocktail waitresses. The other waitresses and I refused to wear those ridiculous outfits, and as people were pouring in the door, we got our way.

The event was a blast to work and the gals who participated were bold, drunk and well-endowed and, yes, wet. They didn't have to do anything other than parade out in front of a mass crowd with loud music blaring and strut their stuff. There was so much energy in the air and everyone drank three times as much as usual, and tipped like they wanted to get rid of all their money.

I have no idea how many more Wet T-Shirt Contests were held after that one, but I'm sure there were many. It's the 21st century now and I can't tell you the last time I saw one advertised in the paper. I'll remind you that it was the '70s and this contest was just another sign of the times—fun and free and, yes, a little crazy.

Full Moon Skiing and Backpacking

Nighttime cross-country skiing under the full moon was a revelation to me being from the flatlands. The snowy mountains under a luminescent full moon are something so special and magical it's hard to describe. No matter how cold it is outside (I put this in the present tense as we still ski in the moonlight), everyone usually gets together for a casual potluck dinner and waits until the moon is out and bright enough to light up the path.

Sometimes there were twenty of us skiing along a tracked trail watching our dogs frolicking in this endless playground. We'd either go to Conundrum, Difficult Campground, Maroon Bells road, Ashcroft or Wildcat. It didn't take long for us to work up a sweat. Off came the hat and then the heavy jacket. The guys of course loved to ski up a steeper slope and have races coming down. We'd come back a couple of hours later with hot, rosy cheeks and bodies that were content. Drinks by the fire at friends' homes near the trails ended these perfect evenings.

Donnie and I were addicted to backpacking. Backpacking was so much a part of our lives that literally the minute the snow melted, we would put away our skis—downhill, telemark and cross-country, ski boots, ski poles—and pull out our Kelty backpacks, which had been stored away for the winter. Except for a few winter cross-country ski trips to the various Braun Huts, our backpacks hung on hooks just waiting to be used again.

Before purchasing these coveted backpacks, we'd spend hours picking out the right one that fit correctly. Nowadays, they're much more high-tech with internal frames and lighter material. But back then, they had a metal structure on which you could bungee-tie your sleeping bag, pad and tent. How the heck we carried all we needed for a few days out in the wilderness is beyond me.

Every time we earned extra money, we purchased an item or two from the R.E.I. catalogue to add to our list of essentials. If we weren't jeeping, we were backpacking with our dogs. Getting out into the mountains was the most fun, often challenging but always an adventure. We loved the fact that we never had to leave our valley to find a new trail. I remember going to: Grizzly Lake, Cathedral Lake, Conundrum Hot Springs, Buckskin Pass, Willow Lake and many more high-country trails.

One time we backpacked Midway Pass starting at the Lost Man Campground up Independence Pass. We had planned on spending two nights out. I thoroughly enjoyed the first few miles of hiking when I'd concentrate on my breathing and footing, beginning to leave the world behind. I'd get lost in the views and the flowers and the rocks and all the incredible beauty right in front of me. Carrying a heavy pack was always a shock to my system until I settled in. Luckily I had purchased really good hiking boots that fit properly and I had broken them in so my feet didn't kill me as they had in the past.

We had a really good long first day and camped when we got tired. That night, one of the dogs surprised a porcupine and wound up with so many quills that he looked like a porcupine himself. Donnie and I were used to the dogs getting stuck with these nasty quills, so we always brought pliers. Donnie would hold the dog down and I'd start plucking them out. To this day, I can still remember the smell of blood as the quills were pulled out, one by one, and the dog became frantic. Because there were so many quills, and the poor dog was in such distress, we could only get a few out. It was very painful for him to lie down and try to sleep. So, no one slept. We got up at the crack of dawn and backpacked all the way down to Hunter Creek in one day instead of two more leisurely days on the trail.

As much as we hated to spend money going to the veterinarian, we really had no choice and off we went to get that poor dog some relief. We wound up back at the Agate with ice packs on our aching backs. And yet, there we were, planning our next trip.

Hiking to Crested Butte

Summers I spent hiking with Donnie but fall was my time to hike with my girlfriends. But I need to digress for a moment. One of my favorite friends was Al Cluck, a true character. I met Al in 1969. I had hitchhiked from Denver to ski in Aspen for a winter weekend. A nice family picked me up near Vail and dropped me off in front of Carl's Pharmacy with my Girl Scout backpack, my Chevron skis with Cubco bindings, and my lace-up ski boots.

I didn't have a clue where I'd stay the next two nights, but a very old, topless, maroon Jeep pulled up to where I was standing. What I noticed in the passenger seat were two beautiful, very large, black, white and gray Siberian Huskies with startling blue eyes—dogs I'd never seen in Illinois. The driver had a mischievous grin and he was a charmer. He was also not a college student! Smiling at me he said hello and introduced himself as Al and asked why I looked so lost. I explained my situation and he immediately told me to jump in with my gear and that I was welcome to join him and his friends for dinner at his place and the couch was mine.

I was naïve but somehow I totally trusted this guy. Al and I became fast friends—he was like an older brother to me. He was an amazing storyteller and mesmerized me with his many hunting tales. Characters like Al existed for me only in books and movies. He was the quintessential mountain man—he was the real deal. That first night he cooked venison meat from a deer he had hunted that fall, butchered and stored for the winter. I had never tasted such tender meat, and I certainly wasn't used to a guy cooking dinner. He also whipped up mashed potatoes and put together a salad.

Al's day job was the P.E. teacher at the old elementary school (the present Yellow Brick) but his passion was being in the outdoors. Al was the guy who opened my world to the many hikes in the Aspen and Snowmass areas. He knew the mountains like the back of his hand. He was the modern Grizzly Adams.

My girlfriend Teri and I had heard Al talk on and on about a cool hike over East Maroon Pass to Crested Butte, a tiny ski town. So in the fall of 1972 Teri and I decided to go on an adventure. We planned and packed well, or so we thought. Al had to leave town unexpectedly so instead of giving us his topographical map of the area and his compass, we only had a vague idea of the route.

Besides Al, we didn't know anyone who had done this hike. It's not like now when all summer and fall, East and West Maroon Passes are frequented with hikers going back and forth. If you hurt yourself nowadays, someone would be by soon. But back then it was a novelty. Instead of getting a ride from Al in his Jeep, we had to hitchhike up to the lake at the base of the Maroon Bells. We helped each other get our heavy backpacks on and stupidly tried to find the trail on the east side of the lake where there isn't a trail. There was no one to ask. Not exactly a great way to begin.

Finally we found the trail that went back down a couple of miles toward town, crossed the river, and we were on our way up East Maroon. We had, however, wasted precious time. Then there were the river crossings and several times we took wrong turns.

It didn't break our spirits. Hiking in the fall along a trail laden with golden aspen leaves and smelling the earthy fragrance is a gift. Walking in the woods surrounded by aspen trees, spruce trees and pine trees and being away from the world always amazes me. When the wind blows and the leaves start falling off the trees, we always yell out "fall foliage" with joy. Then there are the views. No matter how far you've walked, the vistas in the mountains are why people climb and hike. They stop you dead in your tracks because they're so spectacular. You feel small and very lucky to be alive.

We camped that night below the steep switchbacks going to the top of the pass. We could see that we were on the correct path and all was well. The next morning after a great breakfast of French toast, which we cooked on my little stove, and steamy hot coffee, we took off and reached the top of the pass with gorgeous views and a sense of pride and accomplishment (and a mental note to bring the damn map next time!).

We hiked down the other side to Copper Lake and knew that the little ghost town of Gothic was not too far away. Al told us we could catch a ride into Crested Butte from there. But, it was a Tuesday and I think Al was referring to a weekend day. And it was 1972. There were no cars and no people and no cell phones. So we walked and walked on a dirt road. It took us the entire day until finally an old rusty green pickup truck stopped and picked us up a few miles from the ski area and dropped us off at the outskirts of town. We were exhausted but luckily the young man in the truck had some extra water that we gulped down gratefully. As we drove, he explained that the town of Crested Butte historically mined hard rock and coal, and in the 1800s a geologist referred to Crested Butte Mountain and Gothic Mountain as the crested buttes. It was all beautiful and very different from Aspen. This nice guy laughed as we took off our hiking boots and socks and started rubbing out feet—he couldn't believe how far we had walked.

We got out and thanked him profusely. He told us to check out the Forest Queen hotel for a room. The town was only a few blocks long, and the main road was dirt. The storefronts seemed out of the 1800s and we loved it. Very funky! We must have looked a bit odd—two barefoot hippie chicks with long braids and hiking boots dangling off our huge backpacks. People started asking us where we were from and when we told them Aspen, they also couldn't believe we had hiked over the mountain and beyond. Whatever made us want to do that? At some point we felt like mountaineering celebrities and started answering, "because it's there."

Some people followed us as we slowly made our way through town, a scene that now reminds me of the movie, *Forrest Gump*, made in 1994 when Forrest walked with crowds trailing behind him. The folks from Crested Butte were asking us more and more questions. A lady from the local paper interviewed us and took our photo. People led us into bars along the main drag and offered us drinks. I'm pretty sure by then we had started to embellish our two-day adventure. Perhaps we warded off a bear and a mountain lion—honestly I can't remember, but I do remember the

lady at the Forest Queen gave us a room on the house, and someone invited us out for a free pizza dinner. We were amazed at how Crested Butte welcomed us. We loved it so much we stayed four more days and jumped at the chance when some nice soul offered to drive us back to Gothic for the trek back to Aspen.

Harvey, ZG-4074

The next summer arrived and I had saved enough money to purchase my very first car. I really wanted a Jeep from the 1940s. I'd wait to see "for sale" signs in various Jeep windows and inquire. They were either in major need of repair or too expensive. I finally drove to Denver with Bev in her Jeep as she needed to get to the Denver airport. I was happy to see the selection in a big city was plentiful.

Dave Wells, a good buddy of mine from high school and DU, and I ran around Denver for two full days until we found "the one." I fell in love with the price, the red leather seats, and best of all, the carburetor that stuck out of a hole in the hood. With Dave's help, we negotiated a price I could handle—$400. It was a green 1948 Willys, a true classic. The only problem with my newly named Jeep, "Harvey," was that he didn't go over 40 miles an hour. Bev kindly loaned me her Jeep to go back home, and I towed Harvey back to Aspen via Independence Pass. I arrived home and Donnie pointed out how lucky I was as there were only two threads left on the trailer hitch—somehow the rest were stripped away. I could only imagine how horrified I would have been if Harvey had come loose on one of those steep switchbacks on the Pass. I might have died then and there if my new prized possession had fallen off the mountainside. Lucky for me, "he" didn't.

The City of Aspen was pretty lax in those days—no parking meters, and people parked anywhere they wanted. I proudly parked Harvey on the lawn right in front of the Agate along with Bev and Donnie's CJ5 Jeep.

Donnie approved of Harvey, and the dogs immediately peed on his tires to christen him and jumped in the front seat to claim their new home. We spent many wonderful hours in that Jeep. However, Harvey often needed a little TLC and fixing of various old parts. I luckily met "No Problem" Joe working at Buttermilk one day. "No Problem" was an old

man and very skinny. He seemed like a nice grandfather who might have lived in the Smoky Mountains; he was born in Oklahoma in 1912. He dressed with baggy jeans or overalls and an old work shirt. He wore glasses and his face was chiseled and grizzled like a road map. He was from a different era and time and he was incredibly nice to me. After all, I had met many like him in Lenado. I was told they called him "No Problem" because anytime anyone asked him to fix anything, he answered, "No problem." I came to his old wooden cabin by Herron Park with an ailing Harvey. His yard was cluttered with old cars, discarded tools and license plates. Lucky for me, he came to my aid more times than I can tell you. He was very well known around town.

"No Problem" Joe Candreia passed away in 1993 but is immortalized forever with his namesake—the Neale Avenue Bridge was quickly renamed, "No Problem Bridge," and "No Problem" trail leads from East Hopkins Avenue to Herron Park, a connector to the Rio Grande trail. And, there's a cabin on Buttermilk with a sign above the door telling you "No Problem" is not to be forgotten. To the side of that cabin is a ski run named after him. I think about him every time I cruise down it.

That winter my three cousins, aunt and uncle from Larchmont, New York, came out to visit. My cousins loved Harvey and wanted to drive around town again and again with the music blaring. My aunt couldn't figure out how the novelty of driving an old Jeep with no top in the middle of the winter was fun. One day, I drove them back to their condo after dinner. Suddenly I stopped, took the broom handle from its hole in the back, and checked the gas level. My uncle, a New York corporate lawyer, was incredulous. It's a good thing I didn't take them up to Lenado for a tour!

The Rose Lady

Now that I had a car, I had to earn a little more money than usual to pay for insurance, repairs and gas. I was working odd jobs, but one day my sweet neighbor Teri asked if I would fill in for her that evening selling roses as she had the flu and a high fever. Sure, I thought, why not? Anything to help a neighbor.

She loaned me a cute outfit because she said the "Rose Lady" needed to look the part. I wore her beautiful long Victorian skirt; a lacy top and a blazer. I cut the fragrant roses' thorns, placed them in Teri's special rose basket and headed out to hit up all the male diners at the restaurants in downtown Aspen. I was to sell the roses for a dollar each and could keep all the tips I made.

I first walked into the Chart House and couldn't believe that I actually had to interrupt people while they were eating and ask if the guy wanted to buy a rose. I hadn't really thought about this part of the gig. Luckily, the bartender spotted me standing at the entrance, virtually frozen with a basket of roses, and offered me a free shot of tequila. I didn't drink tequila and had never had a shot of anything, but desperate times call for desperate measures, so I downed it like a pro. The transformation was unbelievable. I miraculously regained my composure and confidence, although I found all I really wanted to do was have another shot.

I walked into the main dining room with Teri's beautifully woven basket filled with dark red roses and caught the eye of a man (obviously on a date). He waved me over and I surprised myself by asking in a very sweet British-accented voice, "Would you like a rose for the lady?" "Yes," he said with a smile, "a rose for the lady." Boy, this was easy. After that, guys were waving me over to their tables and the tips were better than cocktail waitressing. It seemed the guys wanted to show off and tipped me way beyond what I expected.

I felt like Cupid, seeing all the women instantaneously fall a little more in love with their man for buying her a rose. If she hadn't been smiling when I arrived, suddenly, with a gorgeous rose or two in her hand, she was glowing. And I was too. I was flushed from the tequila and giddy at how fun the night was. Seven restaurants later, I had sold all 75 roses. I made 90 dollars in tips in an hour. I had hit the motherlode!

The next day I knocked on Teri's door and asked how she was feeling, but sort of hoping she wasn't up to selling that night. She was still not feeling great and had no energy. Would I mind going again? Hell yes, I wouldn't mind at all. I was envisioning a new top for Harvey or maybe some new wheels.

Again, I had another stellar evening. A bartender at the Ute City Banque bought me a drink. I had no idea you could get free drinks by selling roses independently—another great benefit to this newly discovered job. Restaurant by restaurant, table by table, I gained more confidence and was able to scope out the men I was sure would buy a rose. More fabulous tips.

Later that evening when I went back to the Agate and we were all hanging out, a light bulb went off in my brain. Okay, I knew Teri was

moving back to New York soon and there would no longer be a Rose Lady. Couldn't I get a business license and find a flower wholesaler and start my own business? I talked to some friends who said it was doable so I created "Aspen Rosary" and was up and rolling in two weeks.

I bought an old refrigerator at a garage sale and was given tall plastic buckets to keep the flowers happily watered and upright. I found a company in Denver who could sell me the roses wholesale. The roses were bused up to Aspen (yes, the Greyhound Bus came through Aspen in those days) once a week in large, insulated boxes. The roses stayed fresh and beautiful as long as I treated them kindly.

I have to say it was one of the very best jobs I could have ever wished for. I know I keep saying how awesome my jobs were in Aspen, but this was mine and I worked for myself, and it was easy, and I made people happy. Some nights I'd sell the entire contents of my basket within the first fifteen minutes and be invited to sit down to dinner with the group that bought them. Is this for real? I'd ask myself on many occasions. I had to pinch myself.

The Arya was a restaurant in the old Aspen Inn and had several private dining areas where groups could dine and create as much of a ruckus as they desired. I'd knock on the wall next to the curtain to announce I was coming in. Some groups had the telltale mirror on the table with lines of cocaine to be snorted at will. The amount of money they spent in one night on this popular high-inducing designer drug could have paid my rent for six months. But, they had the money so there you have it. It sure didn't bother me as the guys almost always bought roses for all the ladies and tipped me ridiculous amounts of money.

Nowadays, many famous people have their own private chefs flown in to cook for them in their multimillion-dollar homes so as not to be spotted and hassled in restaurants around town. But in the '70s, movie stars, musicians, politicians and others in the spotlight hung out in the local restaurants. They, too, were mere mortals and bought roses, often to my astonishment and delight. I won't mention names but they were generally very kind and I somehow wasn't too starstruck!

The highlight (and there were many) of my rose-selling career

occurred one evening when I was at David Michael's Ute City Banque—
on the corner of Galena Street and Hyman Avenue. I walked up to a table
on the upper level and almost croaked—it was Dr. Burkey, my DU sociology professor whom I had admired so much. I never missed one of his
classes. He immediately bought several roses for his wife. He gave me the
supreme compliment. He suggested I was probably using more of my
education in a positive way than half of his students and certainly having
more fun.

Herman and Lulu Gasser leased Guido's restaurant at the corner of
Cooper Avenue and Galena Street. Herman was well known for being a
gruff, unsentimental and demanding boss. He was always by the bar when
I entered and immediately and graciously bought his wife and all his waitresses a rose. A softie, after all.

Selling roses became a game to me: Walk into a restaurant and figure out who would buy and who wouldn't. I was usually 90 percent correct. I could have written an entire book about those nightly stops, the
people I met and their stories.

I sold roses on the busy nights—usually Thursday, Friday and Saturday. Although, holidays were always profitable, I did a huge business on
St. Patrick's Day by buying green tinted carnations and selling après ski
from the deck of the old Little Nell (before it was remodeled). Combining
selling flowers with drinking all kinds of green drink concoctions was a
perfect match. Talk about selling out quickly. There's nothing like selling a
gimmick to inebriated skiers wanting to party.

Valentine's Day, of course, was the best night of my year. I had to go
home and restock several times. I started getting pre-orders. Business was
so good, I took orders from the Snowmass Ski Patrol by telling the guys
that when they presented their sweethearts a gorgeous bouquet of flowers, they'd for sure get lucky that evening.

Presto! I tripled my orders. I got nice florist paper, wrapped up the
roses or red carnations with pretty greens, stapled cute cards on with red
ribbons and delivered them to the patrolmen's locker room at the end of
the day. The guys were thrilled and gave me nice tips. Then, I'd run home
and get my basket ready for the romantic evening's restaurant runs.

You Mean I Get Paid to Do This?

That summer, Donnie told Bev and me that Teddy Armstrong was looking to set up a summer City gymnastics program at the Elementary School gym in the West End (now referred to as the Yellow Brick). I had loved gymnastics in high school and had taught the younger students after school so I was thrilled. The three of us set up the schedule and figured out how to rotate the kids so they could use the different types of equipment.

The program was very popular—kids love to hang, straddle, do headstands and flip in the air. I remember almost all the kids who were enrolled wanted to be there. We had a large trampoline that the kids found magical and fought to stay on as long as possible. Nowadays, they have belts that go around your waist to help the learning process, but back then, it was trial and error and those kids could not get enough. We had to "spot" them really well as the small kids sometimes bounced so high they almost flew off the tramp.

The boys were very competitive so climbing the rope to touch the ceiling was a big goal for many. Some boys were like monkeys and climbed up with no problem but the chunkier guys really struggled and avoided this challenge at all costs. Donnie also taught the pommel horse. Both the rope and the horse were just for boys.

We spent hours teaching the kids somersaults (forward and backward), handstands, cartwheels, headstands, back handsprings and back walkovers. They put their hearts and souls into learning—they tried over and over to tackle these challenges. We had old mats and all you could hear was the sound of the mats crunching while the kids performed their tumbling skills.

In high school, my forté was the uneven bars. How I loved learning new tricks and being so far off the ground. Uneven bars are just for girls,

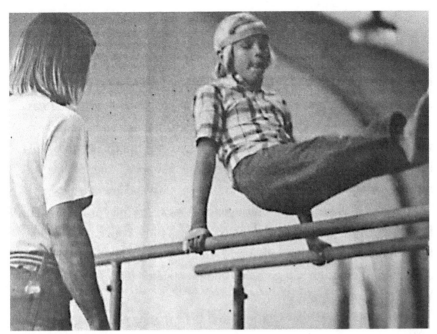
Donnie teaching the youth of America.

and my girls waited in long lines for their turn. Once you learn the basics, you truly feel like you're flying, flipping from one bar to the other with (of course) perfect form.

We worked with both genders on the difficult balance beam. The beam is only four inches wide, which is very intimidating. And then you need to learn how to look straight ahead and still walk forward and backward with your arms out for balance. After learning the basics, the kids would learn more and more difficult mounts, tricks and dismounts. Focus and concentration were key on the beam.

We had an end-of-the-summer demonstration for the kids' parents. The girls got all dressed up in colorful leotards and the boys in gym shorts and T-shirts. We moved from the tramp to the uneven bars, the parallel bars, the pommel horse, the rope and onto the mat for their floor routines. All the parents cheered enthusiastically for every child and the kids loved the attention. Some kids were nervous and some performed with superhuman powers that we didn't know they possessed. Yet another job where, "You mean I get paid to do this?"

On a personal note, I recently ran into the Prior sisters and they clearly remembered as seven- and nine-year-olds being in our gymnastics program along with Etta Skaeringsson. Tina (now called Bailey) said her hero was Olga Korbut, the tiny darling Russian gymnast from the 1974 summer Olympics who earned four gold and two silver medals. She was so cute with her pigtails and red ribbons. Her flexibility and strength wowed everyone. Bailey said our program gave her the chance to be just like her idol, Olga. She recalled our "extreme patience." She told me she had a huge fear of falling but felt "safe, protected and loved."

Lisa said when she was on the uneven bars, she felt "proud and confident" when she finally learned to straddle from the high bar to the low bar and loved the way her little body felt in space as she did pullovers and casts. She said they'd go home and practice on fences around their West End home.

Some 45 years later, I appreciated their sharing these memories with me. It was rewarding to know that we had given these kids a fun and long-lasting experience.

After we ran the summer program, it moved to the larger Red Brick gym and became a year-round program with wonderful coaches, and continues to be extremely popular. The kids now travel to compete and take their gymnastics very seriously. Who knows, maybe we'll have the next Olga Korbut!

Behind the Bar

Winter of 1976 found me bartending at the Main Buttermilk restaurant from noon till the place shut down well after après ski. That is, the "old" restaurant before it became Bumps. It was built in 1958 and designed by local architect Jack Walls. It had a hyperbolic paraboloid roof (a double-curved surface that resembled the shape of a saddle) that rested on two supports and covered 2,000 square feet. It was walled in glass. It was a unique design for the '50s in Aspen. René Baudat was a hardworking Frenchman who ran the cafeteria, shop and bar. He never took a day off and he never got sick.

I knew all the drinks since I had cocktail-waitressed and I had studied the book on how to make Harvey Wallbangers, White Russians, Tequila Sunrises, Screwdrivers and other oddly named drinks. Our customers usually drank beer or hot buttered rum, which we were famous for. René would come behind the bar around 4 p.m. to help out when we had

our rush. We had no time to think. We made drinks with both hands. We never measured but we poured and mixed and were a great team. It slowed down around 5:30 p.m. and René would call out "Last call for alcohol" in his French accent. And he was serious. He arrived at the restaurant at 6:30 a.m. every morning, so by 6 p.m., he was ready to go home.

Buttermilk was host to a group of local ski instructors who were happy, fun-loving, and like the ski patrol, all had colorful names: Toad,

Frog, Bullwinkle, Lizard, Bozo, Warthead and Sarge, to name a few. After teaching either privates to adult beginners or group lessons for kids, they all stopped off at the bar to have a couple of drinks and laugh about their day. They knew one another very well and they knew how to get each other's goat. They knew all the buttons to push to get the late afternoon going in one direction or another. There was never a dull moment.

That was the famous winter of no snow. Although the skiing was not very good, one of our best friends, John Hanson (aka Philly) decided to take advantage of this bizarre winter and invited us over almost every morning for an elaborate breakfast of omelets, pancakes, eggs done every way and either mimosas or Bloody Marys. Philly was a college-educated lift operator on Aspen Mountain and it was the "good old days" when all the locals knew all the longtime lift operators by name and greeted them before loading the slow-moving chairlifts. Philly is the nephew of Holly and Joe Coors (yes, *that* Coors) and was housesitting their beautiful home in the historical West End. After a leisurely breakfast we'd head over to Buttermilk with our rock skis and do our very best to not worry about the lack of snow.

Once you realized there's still nowhere else on earth you'd rather be, all was well in the world. We were just happy to be outside enjoying the sunshine, the good energy of the mountains and the empty slopes.

Music in Aspen

Oh, and then there was the music of the '70s. How could I write this little book without including the music? It was and is so much a part of our lives.

Of course, there was the mainstream music we all loved and listened to: Buffalo Springfield, Bob Dylan, Joan Baez, The Eagles, Jefferson Airplane, Santana, James Taylor, Crosby Stills Nash & Young, Judy Collins, Jimi Hendrix, The Moody Blues and so many more.

We in Aspen were lucky to have so many talented musicians who lived here and played in small and large venues in our valley. Who could forget the Deaf Camp picnics? These were all-day concerts that left you wanting more and usually very sunburned!

One of my favorite places to listen to music was Jake's Abbey, downstairs from Jake's restaurant in a dark, cozy space that was usually jam-packed with musicians and listeners. There was a cover charge at the

The Nitty Gritty Dirt Band

door. My good friend Kurt Brown (Aspen poet and writer) was bartending at Jake's at the time and offered me a job as a cocktail waitress so I could make some money and be surrounded by music two nights a week.

On any given night most of my friends crammed in there to listen to anyone who happened to be playing. I'm sure there were many more, but my favorites were: Bobby Mason and Starwood, Jimmy Buffett, Danny and

Penny Wheetman, Jan and Vic Garrett and their band Liberty, Chris Cox, Dan Forde, John Oates (of Hall & Oates), John Sommers, Steve Martin, and Cecilio and Kapona.

On a personal note: Bobby Mason has been playing music in Aspen since the '60s. I have to say that he is one of the most generous guys on the planet. Whenever someone needs money, Bobby will play a benefit concert—any time, any place. Plus he's an awesome man, father, husband (he's now married to my college buddy Jane Beckwith), friend and music maker.

In the summers, Aspen Music Festival students came here to study, play in the orchestra at the old Music Tent and around town, similar to what they do today. There's nothing better than sitting outside the Tent, spreading out a blanket with a lovely picnic and listening to music.

Bands played at The Little Nell (The Gallery back then), The Blue Moose, The Inn at Aspen, The Pub, Rock 'N Horse (below the Hotel Jerome), and basically all around Aspen. Snowmass brought us to the Timbermill and the Tower—often to hear Twirp Anderson and Cash Cashman. We danced and danced, even after skiing all day long and often in our ski boots.

OF NOTE: I was reminded that the original Eagles band played their first gig here in 1971 at The Gallery in the old Little Nell. They performed in our little mining town before releasing their first album and before reaching super stardom. Don Henley bought a home in Woody Creek and Glenn Frey bought a home near Jimmy Buffett on the Snowmass Creek Road. They loved to play music and party here in Aspen.

We had our own bands who became famous: The Nitty Gritty Dirt Band with Jimmy Ibbotson, Bobby Mason and Starwood, Liberty, Black Pearl, and, of course, John Denver.

I guess everyone has a John Denver story. Here's mine: When I first met Donnie, we'd drive around Aspen in his Jeep with no top and the windshield down on the hood and he'd have his eight-track tape player booming out music for one and all to hear. I was very much into Janis Joplin at the time. Donnie played John Denver constantly. I had never heard of him before, and to be honest, I wasn't into the down-home country songs. One day, we were going jeeping up to the Crystal Mill and

CHRIS COX

I brought one of my Joplin tapes. But it sat on the floor as John sang to us for hours—I guess the driver got to pick the music!

After we moved to Lenado, Donnie surprised me by buying two tickets to Paepcke Auditorium for a midnight concert with—none other than John Denver. Oh boy, I thought, this may be the end of a lovely relationship. I'm a nice person and didn't want to be rude so after a delicious lobster dinner and Barbara's famous hot fudge sundaes at The Steak Pit, we walked over to Paepcke on a cold, moonlit night.

I sat down in my seat and—lo and behold—a dog was sitting next to me. A real live golden retriever was sitting in the next seat with his owner next to him. The owner introduced me to Jack and asked if I liked dogs and I told him, as I was petting Jack, that I loved dogs. He went on to tell me that Jack loved John Denver and so, since his date bowed out of the concert, he brought Jack. That sounded logical to me.

The concert started with Bill and Taffy Danoff who are singer/songwriters. They performed several songs that I thoroughly enjoyed. Then the lights dimmed and John came onstage playing his guitar and it crescendoed louder and louder and Jack and I were on the edges of our chairs while John sang "The Eagle and The Hawk." I had chills running throughout my body. The song is so powerful.

And the concert went on from there. Danoff had written, "I Guess He'd Rather Be in Colorado" and "Take Me Home, Country Roads," which they all sang together. John sang many songs from his new album, *Poems, Prayers and Promises.* I quit comparing him to Janis. I became a fan that night, and Donnie and I went to all his Aspen concerts in the Music Tent,

Liberty

the Wheeler Opera House and many other venues. Never again did a dog sit next to me.

The concert lasted over two hours, and after awhile I just felt as if I was in someone's living room. I never got tired. Jack, however, fell sound asleep and rested his head in my lap.

On a personal note: John loved to ski. He skied Snowmass quite often and, for some reason, he met Donnie and enjoyed skiing with the patrol boys. One day, I was skiing with Donnie and the boys and there was John. I have never seen a happier guy on skis. He literally grinned from ear to ear and had this great laugh. We skied a lot of secret spots and John was beyond thrilled.

We heard Taffy and Bill Danoff perform one more time in Aspen. Sadly, it was at the Music Tent in 1997 for John's beautiful and music-filled Celebration of Life. John was killed when his small experimental plane crashed into the Pacific Ocean.

Over the years, many of our musicians have died or moved away. Many remain here today and continue to perform. We're so grateful they graced our lives in Aspen for so many amazing years. Luckily, we have some new voices to enjoy. Life goes on.

Ted Bundy

People in small towns can collectively freak out about certain things, and having a handsome, charismatic serial killer, rapist and kidnapper who had just escaped our historic courthouse qualified as one.

Theodore "Ted" Bundy had been quietly and confidently murdering young women in seven states over the course of four years, from 1974-1978. More than creepy was that Ted decapitated at least a dozen of his victims. He was good looking so when he approached young, naïve women asking for help, they were only too happy to comply. He'd have his arm in a sling and ask a young woman to help him bring a canoe (or whatever heavy object he couldn't carry on his own) to his VW Beetle, and then they'd disappear without a word.

We in Aspen became aware of Bundy's evilness January 12, 1975, when Caryn Campbell (23), a nurse staying at the Wildwood Inn in

Snowmass Village, disappeared while walking down a well-lit outside hall-way between the elevator and her room. Her nude body was found a month later on a dirt road just three miles away from the Snowmass hotel. Two months later, Julie Cunningham (26), a Vail ski instructor disappeared while walking from her Vail apartment to town for dinner. Bundy admitted years later he approached her on crutches (another of his little tricks) and asked her to carry his ski boots to his car where he assaulted and handcuffed her, drove her to Rifle and strangled her to death. Bundy was beyond diabolical, beyond gruesome.

Weeks later, April 6, Denise Oliverson (25) disappeared in Grand Junction. May 10, Bundy drowned and sexually assaulted 12-year-old Lynette Culver in Idaho. And his brutal killing spree went on and on, unbeknownst to us in Aspen.

Ted was arrested at a routine traffic stop August 1975 by a Utah Highway Patrolman. Even though they found all sorts of incriminating evidence in his VW—a pantyhose mask, crowbar, handcuffs, an ice pick and more, he was let go. Really? Did the patrolman think he was going to a costume ball? What a travesty that the patrolman missed finding photos of Bundy's poor victims he had in his car.

Later, several detectives and prosecutors met in Aspen from five states and were finally convinced Bundy was the evil force behind so many of these brutal murders. In March 1976, Bundy was found guilty of the kidnapping and assault of one girl who survived, and he was sentenced to one to fifteen years in the Utah State Prison.

Bundy was then transferred to Aspen in June 1977 to stand trial for Caryn Campbell's murder. This is when it all becomes too bizarre. Bundy served as his own attorney (he was a law school dropout) and was excused by the judge from wearing handcuffs or leg shackles. Are you kidding me? Bundy is on the FBI's Ten Most Wanted Fugitives list and our judge lets him roam free? Yes, and during a recess, he gets permission to go to the law library, opens a window and jumps from the second story to freedom. No Hollywood script could have been written with a more ironic twist.

I had been following the story since poor Caryn Campbell was

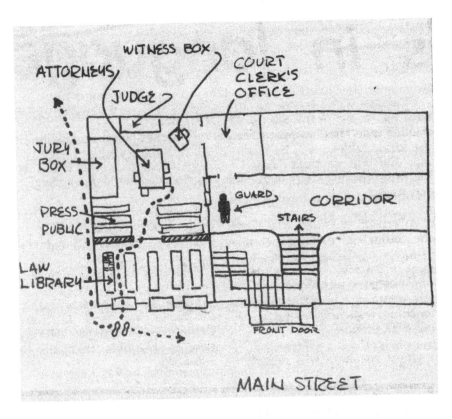

Labels in image: WITNESS BOX, ATTORNEYS, COURT CLERK'S OFFICE, JUDGE, JURY BOX, GUARD, CORRIDOR, PRESS, PUBLIC, STAIRS, LAW LIBRARY, FRONT DOOR, MAIN STREET

murdered two years before. Most of us in Aspen were horrified that he had actually been here in Snowmass. We now took it personally. And here he was, this evil guy loose in our quaint little town. I'm not sure about the guys, but we gals were all scared. We looked over our shoulders, we locked our doors, and we carried mace for protection—just in case. We all knew his M.O., and he knew we knew so he was on the down low. Plus, he now was an escapee on the run.

I was very aware that he liked girls with long brown hair, parted down the middle. I fit that description back then, so I was even more nervous. I totally would have been one of those innocent girls that would have fallen for his little act of asking for help while on crutches or with his arm in a sling. But now I was frightened and felt like I did when I was 15, and Richard Speck murdered eight student nurses in Chicago. With all the press (TV and news media) surrounding these horrible atrocities, everyone was filled with fear. Our parents talked to us about self-defense and reminded us to be aware at all times. I think Richard Speck's inhumanity made me lose some of my innocence.

I grew up just a few blocks from the Chicago border. I lived in a house with a vacant lot next door and nothing good happened there after midnight. Lots of guys hung out there to drink and smoke pot and get loud. I was often awakened in the middle of the night with guys yelling and running around our front yard. I also had some scary experiences baby-sitting and hitchhiking, so being frightened was nothing new to me. I survived a robbery in our house in college as well as a freaky peeping Tom.

That summer in '77, I was a hostess at one of the brand-new Aspen Club Condos. I'd wait for Realtors to bring by prospective clients and then I'd give them the detailed tour. It was a Sunday afternoon and Bundy was still missing. I had given four tours that morning, but by 2 p.m., I hadn't seen anyone for a couple of hours so I sat outside on the sunny deck reading a book about Charles Manson. Yes, true fact. The managers of the Aspen Club were Sally and Marv Huss, and they lived on the property but were in Denver for the weekend. They had two huge Newfoundland dogs that were very quiet most of the time. It was peaceful there, in spite of my book's subject, with the river running behind the condos and the birds chirping. Suddenly, the dogs started barking like wild animals. I was gripped with fear. Their barking was so out of the norm. I could only assume there was either a bear or a human trespasser.

I ran into the condo and locked all the doors and closed all the windows. I could hear the dogs and their high-pitched, never-take-a-breath barking for more than an hour. I had walked to work, a mile from town. There was no phone in the condo—and no cell phones back then. My heart was pounding so hard I could hear it. The place had no curtains over the windows. I just knew it was Bundy and that he had scoped me out—I fit the description as I said earlier. I knew Bundy was hiding out until he could tear down the door and murder me. So I did what any young terrified girl would do if she thought these were her last hours on earth: I grabbed a heavy fireplace iron and hid under the master bed. There were no knives in the kitchen (it was just a model condo). I waited

and waited. I prayed.

No one came to my rescue. True, I wasn't late in returning home so no alarms went off in Donnie's mind. Finally, the dogs quit barking and eventually I crawled out from under the bed and waited until my gut told me I was safe. I hurried home to tell my harrowing tale to anyone who would listen.

And still, they didn't find Bundy. The police set up a roadblock and searched everyone's cars and trunks as people exited town. Can you imagine? I'm sure many in the courthouse (including the judge) that day had their heads rolling. After all, they weren't dealing with a drug dealer—no, it was Bundy. How could he possibly have escaped so easily? The question was on all of our minds.

Donnie and I lived on one side of a duplex on the golf course with another couple. We owned a '72 Porsche 911 that we had bought from a friend who needed to sell it immediately for cash. We got such a good deal, we couldn't refuse. Donnie had always wanted a little sports car. This friend showed us how to shift gears, as it was tricky, and taught us all its other idiosyncrasies.

A Sunday night, several days after my Aspen Club scare, Donnie and I were exhausted after a long hike and were sound asleep when Brandy and Killy barked briefly. Donnie got up and looked around but soon went back to sleep.

The next morning we heard it on the news: Bundy was captured up Independence Pass in a stolen car. Wow, what a relief. I went outside and looked at our Porsche and realized something was wrong. First, it was further down the driveway from where we had left it and, second, it was in neutral. We always left it in gear, as the emergency brake was unreliable. Third, it wouldn't start. The battery was dead because not only had the lights been left on but the key was in the ignition in the "on" position. This was weird because we hadn't driven it that night. I was running into the house when our neighbor came up to me and said that Bundy had stolen their car. It was their Cadillac he was driving when the cops stopped him driving up Independence Pass. Two deputies noticed a car weaving and pulled it over, assuming a drunk driver was behind the wheel. Bingo, it was Bundy. Finally.

Meanwhile, heart-thumping panic set in when I realized our car was parked next to our neighbors'. Ted Bundy, the escapee, serial murderer had been at our house, in our car and, he had tried to steal *our* car but couldn't figure out how to get it into reverse (one of the trickiest parts of the stick shift).

I ran inside to tell Donnie and our roommates. I was about ready to call the police and see if they wanted to fingerprint our car, but Donnie calmly said that since they caught him red handed, they'd have a lot more on their plates than coming over to our house. I can get very dramatic and excited while Donnie was always calm, cool and collected.

So, you think the Bundy story is over? No, it is not. Bundy was moved to the Glenwood Springs jail where he pulled a *Shawshank Redemption* scheme. He acquired a hacksaw blade and during the evenings, he sawed a hole in the corner of his cell's ceiling, lost almost 40 pounds and squeezed through the crawlspace. He broke through the ceiling into the jailer's apartment, changed into street clothes and escaped to freedom once again. The jail's crew didn't discover he had escaped until seventeen hours later—just enough time for this monster to steal a car, take a bus and then fly to Chicago.

I'll say it again: Bundy was on the FBI's Ten Most Wanted Fugitive list. Don't you think law enforcement would take him seriously?

From Chicago, Bundy wound up in Tallahassee, Florida, where he terrorized and brutally assaulted several women in a sorority house on the campus of Florida State University. He murdered two of these innocent women, and the others survived. He went on to murder a 12-year-old girl in Lake City, Florida.

Finally, he was arrested February 1978. After many years in court and on death row, Bundy got what he deserved on January 24, 1989 (too bad it took so long)—death by electrocution.

I know it caused a lot of excitement in our little mining town but I often think of all those women and girls who were just going about living their lives and never knew their fates were sealed. I feel terrible for all their families and friends who had to live through the horrors. I wish Bundy had never been born.

I have told my near-miss story many times whenever anyone brings up Ted Bundy at a dinner or cocktail party. Poor Caryn Campbell truly haunted many of my dreams. Women slept better after Bundy's death. The mountains sang a song of solace to us the day he died.

NOTE: It's now 2019 and I just watched *20/20* about Bundy and how he eluded the law for so long. A former FBI profiler said, "We collectively have a fascination with Ted Bundy." Zac Efron is starring as Bundy in *Extremely Wicked, Shockingly Evil, and Vile* on Netflix, a chronicle of his vicious murders. I personally will not watch it.

She Shot Him

Only a year after Ted Bundy murdered Caryn Campbell in Snowmass Village, Claudine Longet became the center of attention and gossip in Aspen. On March 21, 1976, Longet killed her boyfriend and lover, Spider Sabich, with a .22 caliber pistol with just one bullet.

I had only met the outrageously handsome California-surfer-looking World Cup and U.S. Ski Team champion once. But he was always friendly

and said "hi" to me on the streets or on the slopes. Remember the movie, *Downhill Racer*? Robert Redford played Spider. He was a sports hero. Aspen adored him—he was one of our own. A good guy.

Longet was once an actress and singer and had been married to singer Andy Williams and had three children, Noelle, Christian and Bobby. Longet and Spider met in 1972, and by 1975 she and her kids had moved into Spider's lavish Starwood home. But within a year things had soured between the two, and everyone in town knew it.

Spider returned to his home late in the afternoon of March 21, after a training session at Aspen Highlands. He was shot by Longet in the bathroom. She claimed that the gun accidently backfired when Spider was showing her how to use it.

Members of the Pitkin County Sheriff's department made some

errors that helped Longet's defense. Without warrants, they took a blood sample, which showed she had cocaine in her blood, and they took her diary. The gun was mishandled by non-weapons experts. Perhaps because of these errors, Longet was convicted by a jury of a lesser charge: misdemeanor criminal negligence. She served only 30 days in our local jail. The judge allowed her to choose her days and to paint her cell pink.

Longet vacationed with her defense attorney, Ron Austin, who was married at the time. Longet and Austin eventually got married and, as of this writing, remain so. People in Aspen didn't like any of it. However, for months afterwards it created never-ending debates all over town as to what really happened. Spider's death was a loss to Aspen.

On a personal note: I heard through the grapevine that Claudine

Andy Williams and Claudine Longet approaching the Pitkin County Courthouse.

needed someone to live with her children for a month in autumn of 1978 while she went to Europe. I was leery to work for her after all that had happened. However, I needed the money so I applied and got the job. She was nice to me, and I really loved spending time with her three kids. Killer or not, Claudine's kids needed someone to take care of them and I was determined to do the best job I could. They lived in a classic yellow Victorian across from the Music Tent. When the kids were in school, I could cycle to my other job during lunchtime bartending at the Ute City Banque downtown. It ended up being ideal. I loved living in that comfy home. It was off-season, so there was no traffic in this peaceful part of town.

The three kids were full of fun energy. After school let out, we'd ride our bikes, go for beautiful fall hikes in the area or chill out eating popcorn and playing card games. I attended their sporting events, did their laundry, helped with their homework, and demanded they make their beds in the morning.

At first, I cooked them gourmet dinners and packed them creative lunches for school. What I found out was that they were just as happy with boxed mac and cheese. They loved easy American comfort food, so I gave myself a break and quit the fancy dinners.

Every once in awhile, out of the blue, I think of Spider. His legend lives on.

Murder, Cocaine and Steven Grabow

Remember when Aspen was considered the cocaine capital of the entire U.S.? We certainly gained quite the reputation. In the 1970s Police Chief Dick Ritchie brought in an undercover cop to break up a drug ring. He partied with unsuspecting people all over Aspen and then busted many of his new buddies.

We will never forget Steven Grabow who had a perpetual tan, thick, slick, black hair, wore all-white ski suits and drove an immaculately clean black Jeep. From 1984 to 1986 federal agents kept eagle eyes on Grabow whom they assumed was the alleged leader of a drug ring. Late November 1985 Grabow and two other locals and five non-locals were indicted by a federal grand jury. They all pleaded guilty except Grabow. Even so, Grabow was to testify in January in U.S. District Court in Denver for allegedly heading a drug ring that brought 35 million dollars worth of cocaine to Aspen annually.

He never made it to Denver. In December, after playing tennis at the Aspen Club, Grabow was blown up by a pipe bomb that had been placed under the seat of his Jeep. The murder remains a mystery. However, once again, it was fuel for gossip all around Aspen.

On a personal note: I was at the Aspen Club that very day and left the parking lot one hour before Grabow was blown up. These events never cease to amaze me.

The plot thickened again when ten years later, in Arizona, Gary Triano, a real estate developer, was also murdered by a pipe bomb in his car. Many in law enforcement believe that the two murders were related. I won't get into all the webs that were spun, but suffice it to say, CBS' 48 Hours, Dateline, American Greed and Snapped all jumped on this juicy, complicated story.

One-time Aspen resident, former Triano girlfriend and socialite

Grabow Saga Ends in Bomb Blast (Aspen Times front page headline, December 12, 1985). "Federal and local law enforcement officers…inspected the remains of the Jeep in which alleged drug dealer Steven H. Grabow died as it sat in its parked position at the Aspen Club. The car apparently moved a dozen feet or more before a bomb exploded underneath Grabow, although the police would not say what kind of bomb was involved."

Pamela Phillips was charged and sentenced to life in prison for her connection to Triano's murder. Coincidence? We in Aspen kept shaking our heads at all these twists and turns. Life is never boring.

My girlfriends in Illinois always want to know what has happened recently in Aspen, as they don't have these kinds of stories in their worlds. Who does?

Sam's Knob

My good friend Jane Alder (now Dinsmoor) approached me on the street one winter in January and asked if I wanted to waitress with her at the sit-down restaurant on top of Sam's Knob in Snowmass. Jane and I were fellow Stitch and Bitchers and Jane's future husband, Bill, ski patrolled with Donnie on Snowmass Mountain.

Paul and his wife, Hanna, met in Davos, Switzerland, in 1946. The Wirths moved to Aspen in 1948, had five children and ran the Sundeck restaurant (a much smaller structure than it is now) from 1952 to 1966. Paul and Hanna moved over to Snowmass in 1969 to run Sam's Knob.

I had cocktail-waitressed but explained to Jane I had zero experience in food-waitressing. She said, no problem, she'd train me "on the job." Great, as I always needed another job or two.

I showed up to work around 11 a.m. as instructed. It was a beautiful sunny day so Jane told me it might be really busy: Besides the indoor tables, we'd also be serving out on the deck. That meant I'd have more tables than usual. Okay, I thought, let the games begin. Jane handed me an order pad and pen.

NEWS FLASH—MILLENNIALS: This was before the computerized system restaurants use now and makes a waiter or waitresses' job much easier.

All of a sudden, hungry skiers started pouring into the restaurant in droves. Holy Toledo! I still had no idea what to do. Jane walked by me and apologetically said, "You'll do fine." I looked around panicked as the entire restaurant was full inside and out. I took a deep breath and figured it couldn't be that hard. At least I knew which tables were my responsibility, and by then a couple of really nice busboys showed up to help us.

My first table was easy—they all ordered the same thing with Coca-Colas. The next table ordered two bottles of wine to start. Luckily,

the busboys knew the wines and where they were stored. I was not into wines back then so, believe it or not, I had no idea how to open a bottle. I definitely could have used a little lesson on that before the rush but that didn't happen. I quickly figured out how to screw the spiral part into the cork, but even when I put the bottle between my legs (oh, yes I did) to get some leverage to yank the cork out, it hardly moved. I could hear Peter Afholter, the chef, ringing my "food-ready" bell so I simply looked at the man who had ordered the wine and told him I was so sorry but it was my first day and would he mind finishing the job? Before he had time to reply, I put the bottle down in front of him and dashed off to deliver the hot food to another table.

Jane seemed to balance six plates on her arms, but I couldn't figure out her trick so I'd run two plates at a time. And run I did. The "It's my first day at work" line worked so well I used it the rest of the day. Truth be told, I used it the rest of the season. All that running around and trying to figure everything out was exhausting, but the most difficult part was trying to calculate the table's check when I had to keep referring to the prices on the menu. Oh, and checks didn't automatically calculate the

correct tax like they do nowadays. We had to use an old-fashioned calcu-
lator. And we had to manually run the credit cards by keying in the numbers—very time-consuming.

Jane was way too busy for me to ask her for help. After taking forever to do my first check, I just sort of calculated what I thought things
cost, and it all seemed to work out. After my first crazy day, I took the
menu home and studied the items and prices and learned about the
wines so if I was asked a question, I could answer it correctly.

Luckily, skiers for the most part are a mellow group of people and as
long as they have something to quench their thirst right away, they were
patient with my lack of experience. People don't mind a clueless waitress
as long as she apologizes and smiles a lot. Nowadays, I can spot a "me"
right away and sometimes I help bus her tables and I always give her a little extra tip.

I gained confidence and ended up loving that job. I only worked a
couple of days a week but, as I got more proficient, I was able to meet
and chat with many of the regulars. My favorites were the "Top of the
Knob Gang," a group of older men who reserved the private dining room
with the most spectacular view of Mount Daly. They told jokes, shared ski
tales and cherished their testosterone-filled lunch dates.

Jane and the staff called me their "hobby" waitress. I never food-
waitressed again, and I never did open a bottle of wine that season. I had
used my "trick" so often that many of the regulars simply offered to open
the wine before I asked.

DUDLEY'S ON SAM'S KNOB'S
VEGETARIAN CHILI

Do you remember the delicious Dudley's Diner at the Airport Business Center? Patti and Paul Dudley ran this ever-popular restaurant for many years. They took over running Sam's Knob Restaurant from 1991-2000.

Since I was unable to obtain any of Paul or Hanna's recipes, I know Patti's recipe for her hearty chili will not disappoint.

16 ounce can diced tomatoes in juice

16 ounce can pinto beans

16 ounce can kidney beans

16 ounce can black beans

½ cup onions, chopped

½ cup green pepper, chopped

½ cup celery, chopped

½ tsp Tabasco sauce

1 T chili powder

1 T cumin

1 tsp black pepper

2 tsp each: garlic salt, oregano, parsley

1 tsp coriander

Now, get this:

Place everything in a large pot and simmer 1-2 hours.

Serve with fresh bread or corn bread and a tossed salad for a healthy meal.

The Wienerstube

Who can forget the original Wienerstube restaurant—the one that was located in the Aspen Grove Building on Cooper Avenue next to Pinocchio's? Helmut and Gerhard had been boyhood friends in Austria. After apprenticing for three years, they came to Aspen and worked at the Red Onion.

The owner of the Aspen Grove Building was so impressed by these two young men and their cooking skills he talked them into opening their own restaurant in his building. Popular with locals and tourists alike, the "Stube" served one of the best, most consistent breakfasts in town.

A friend told me they were looking for a hostess and the money was great. Music to my ears as I loved working in new establishments and meeting new people and stashing some money in my new savings account. I applied when I found out I didn't have to wear the traditional dirndl the waitresses were required to wear.

I was transitioning out of my hippie stage, but no way was I donning one of those cutesy, colorful Heidi outfits. If any of my friends walked into the Stube while I was working (and they all did) and saw me in one of those costumes, well, let's just say the concept of wearing a nice dress or skirt suited me perfectly!

All the girls were scared of Helmut because he rarely smiled and he barked orders. Luckily for me, Donnie and I had beaten Helmut and his wife Brunhilde in a recent tennis tournament so he actually liked me before I started working and was always kind and considerate. I also realized something about Helmut—he lived with chronic back pain. I often found him lying on the hard floor in the kitchen to alleviate the pressure of being on his feet all day. It was a lifelong lesson for me to try to better understand people before I so quickly judge them.

Gerhard was friendly and great to work for. They trained us and expected efficiency and consistency. I'll always appreciate the many pointers and attention to detail I learned while working there. I loved all the waitresses (dirndls and all). It was hard work but we helped one another and the day passed quickly. The Stube was known for its Eggs Benedict and of course, their large, tasty Bloody Marys. There was always a long wait on Sundays, but no one minded waiting while downing a couple of life-saving Bloodys to nurse a nasty hangover and catch up with others in the same boat.

And who could forget the Stammtisch? The Stube's round joiner table was a vital part of our community. And they say *girls* can talk! I'm here to tell you, so can men. Men of all occupations, from ski instructors to lift operators, to lawyers and everything in between, were welcome to sit down at that table and enter into a lively debate. On several occasions, hands were slammed down trying to make a point. Many of these men came from different countries and when they got really excited, they started speaking in their mother tongue—then you knew the heat was on. Those guys solved many problems and offered a host of solutions—at least while they were sitting there. No matter how intense it got, they always shook hands when they left.

OF NOTE: Summer of 2018 I attended a Wienerstube reunion with many of the wonderful ladies I worked with in the '70s. It was such a treat to reminisce with these women, who came with their husbands or boyfriends and some from as far away as Australia.

WIENERSTUBE'S WIENER SCHNITZEL

Serves 4-8

2 lbs leg of veal, cut into slices, ¼ inch thick

Salt and freshly ground pepper

2 eggs, beaten

½ C flour, enough to coat the Schnitzel on both sides

2 C bread crumbs, homemade using dry French bread

1½ C vegetable shortening

1 lemon

Prepare the slices of veal by lightly pounding them with a meat mallet, or simply marinate them in a squeeze of fresh lemon juice for about an hour in the refrigerator to tenderize the meat. When marinated, pat them dry, then sprinkle with salt and pepper.

Dip in flour and shake off the excess, then dip them in the beaten eggs and lay them flat in bread crumbs. Cover them well with more bread crumbs and press down lightly. Gently shake off any excess.

You can prepare this ahead of time and refrigerate for no longer than 30 minutes.

Heat the shortening in an iron 12-inch skillet until a light haze forms over it. Add the cutlets so they lay flat and don't crowd each other.

Cook over medium heat, turning gently with tongs until crisp and golden brown.

Serve at once with lemon wedges, German potato salad and Lingonberry relish.

Those Were the Days
A PHOTO COLLAGE

While writing this book I enthusiastically pored through The Aspen Times from the 1970s. Near the end of production, I realized I had collected many fun photos and hadn't used them. So I added this Photo Collage to reflect those carefree times.

"Aspen in the 70s was an enchanting time."

—Mari Peyton

Who could forget the Aspen State Teachers College? Marc Demmon ("Dr. Slats Cabbage") and Al Pendorf ("Dean Folton Begley").

"IN A DEMOCRACY PEOPLE USUALLY GET THE KIND OF GOVERNMENT THEY DESERVE — AND THEY DESERVE WHAT THEY GET."

RAOUL DUKE

THOMPSON FOR SHERIFF COMMITTEE — REV. BENTON D.D.

An old-fashioned Fourth of July parade. Notice Crossroads Drug on the corner of Cooper Avenue and Galena Street.

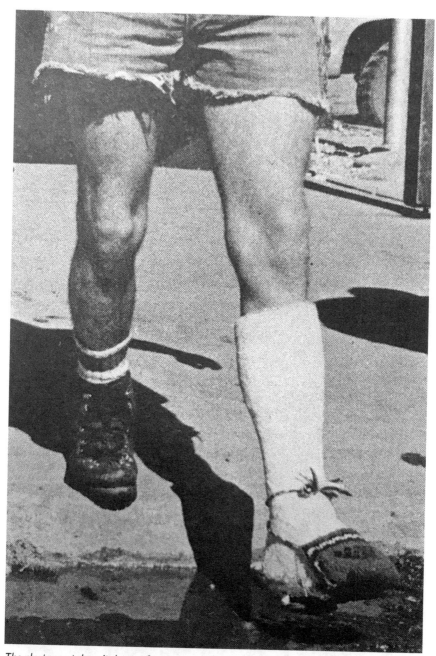

The plaster cast doesn't detract from the great ski legs. Notice the hand-knit toe warmer, a must-have item in the 70s when there's a boo-boo.

Little Annie's
Celebrates its first anniversary
We thank you Aspen

Within the image: CARSON

THE ASPEN TIMES

Vol. No. 90 * No. 32 * Aspen, Colorado 81611
August 12, 1971 * 15 Cents

Installing new lift towers on Aspen Mountain the "easy" way, 1971.

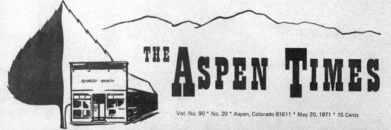

Happy Hearth Inn offered for sale

Story on Page 5-B

THE ASPEN TIMES

Vol. No. 90 * No. 20 * Aspen, Colorado 81611 * May 20, 1971 * 15 Cents

POLICE PUT DAMPER ON CHIMNEY CAPER

(The story in photos inside)

Damson Nakaimi is hauled from the chimney of Carl's Pharmacy early Monday where he was wedged during an apparent burglary attempt.
Photo by Steve Wishart

Aspen police put the damper on a chimney caper at Carl's Pharmacy Monday morning, May 17, when they arrested Damson Nakaimi in the store's fireplace.

Unable to fly the coop, the budding Santa Claus bandit was cooped in the flue when employees arrived at Carl's for work.

Nakaimi had wedged himself into the base of the chimney some six hours earlier while making an abortive attempt at slidding down the chimney with a bag full of tools.

He came to rest at a bend in the flue, with his feet dangling down into the second story fireplace, surrounded by merchandise.

A salesgirl went to her post upstairs and reported hearing muffled sounds.

Investigating, employees discovered a pair of shoes, full, dangling into the store.

Asked what he was doing, Nakaimi said, "I'm looking for my cat. He went down the chimney and I followed him. He must be down there somewhere."

The cat was never found and perhaps it is as well; Nakaimi never explained what he was going to do to the feline with the creel of tools he was carrying.

A crowd of 20-30 people gathered on the street to watch police, lead by Chief Dick Ritchey, pull Nakaimi out of the chimney with a rope.

It had all the excitement and suspense of opening a present, only in this case the question was not 'what is it', but 'who is it?'"

Emerging from the chimney with arms over his head clutching the rescue rope, Nakaimi looked cold and weak as he was delivered from the chimney's firm grip into that of the law.

Nude from the waist up, he had suffered scrapes on the chest, back and arms in his attempts to wriggle free.

He did, however, retain enough strength to raise a defiant middle finger towards a photographer on his way to the ground in the city's utility bucket.

After his arrest, Nakaimi admitted to authorities that he had larcenous intent when he entered the chimney.

He will be charged with burglary and possession of burglary tools, according to the Deputy District Attorney's office.

Although Nakaimi is not accused of taking anything from the store, burglary per se includes the simple penetration of the premises, and under the law, the odd ankle in the chimney is as good as a hand in the till.

Bond in Nakaimi's case has been set at $1300 and charges will be filed in District Court.

Nakaimi is originally from Hawaii, but has lived in the Aspen area since the beginning of the winter.

Nuisance bear trapped near Independence

Wildlife Conservation Officers Mike Stone and Allen Whitaker last week trapped a "nuisance bear" in the Mt. Valley subdivision and released it unharmed in a remote area of the state.

The bear had been invading garbage cans, killing chickens and causing other difficulties for some time. It bit a camper at Difficult Campground last summer and just before it was trapped, reached into a tipi pitched west of Independence Pass.

"A bear reduced to this kind of existence is a degradation to its species," Whitaker said. "We could have had a repeat of the Glacier Park incident if it had not been handled."

Responding to a call, the officers baited a trap — made from a piece of culvert similar to those used in finger towards a photographer on with honey. They were able to trap the cinnamon-colored, adult male animal without any danger of drug overdose, and released it unharmed.

He had "wedged himself into the base of the chimney some six hours earlier while making an abortive attempt at slidding (sic) down the chimney with a bag full of tools." He came to rest at a bend in the flue, with his feet dangling down into the second story fireplace, surrounded by merchandise....."I'm looking for my cat. He went down the chimney and I followed him. He must be down there somewhere," said Damson Nakaimi. Only in Aspen. Only in the 70s.

It's a dog's life

Elizabeth Paepcke, philanthropist and visionary.

Vol. 94 * No. 28 * July 10, 1975 * Aspen, Colorado 81611 * 20 Cents * 3 Sections

THE ASPEN TIMES

Trouble at the Bells

Can people, cars, and wilderness all find happiness in the same square mile?

"Trouble at the Bells." Some things never change...

Relaxing at the Music Tent in the 70s. Tent design by Herbert Bayer, replacing Eero Saarinen's original tent design. Today's tent was designed by Harry Teague.

the parlour car
see next page

The Parlour Car, which housed a complete restaurant serving gourmet meals. It was located literally under the shadow of Shadow Mountain.

horses & bike trails

They're not always compatible, commissioners were told two weeks ago by a group of equestrians. And after a ride along—and sometimes on top of—the newly blacktopped bicycle trail on the Rio Grande right-of-way from Slaughterhouse Bridge into town, commissioners Joe Edwards and Dwight Shellman agreed. Edwards is pointing to the location nearer the Roaring Fork River where the county will cut an entirely separate horse trail thus solving the horse-bike conflict.

Text on sign in image:
1971
WINTERSKOL QUEEN
CANDIDATES
1971 king - DAN DAILEY
1970 queen - SUE SHEASLEY
queen mother -
MYRNA ARMSTRONG

'71s top stories, photos
Inside .....

Making a fast deposit or withdrawal (and that ain't hay) at the Bank of Aspen's drive-up window one day this week was a trot-up customer from the hills.   Photo by Alison Ehrlich

THE ASPEN TIMES

Vol. No. 90 * No. 52 * Aspen, Colorado 81611 * December 30, 1971 * 15 Cents

OLYMPIC BID CONSIDERED

Aspen may have a chance to host the 1976 Olympic Alpine events if the town will support a ski corp bid for the events, city and county officials were told at a special cocktail party Tuesday evening.

Explaining the possibility to two of the three county commissioners and five of the seven members of the City Council was Denver Olympic Committee Member and Aspen Skiing Corp Director F. George Robinson.

On hand to corroborate his statements and to express ski corp approval were D. R. C. Brown, president; Tom Richardson vice president; Curt Burton, marketing director and Art Pfister, a director.

Robinson explained that, although Denver had been awarded the 1976 Winter Olympic Games, there has been an indication that the International Olympic Committee would permit

the Nordic and Alpine events to be held at separate existing resorts within the state.

He pointed out that it would cost roughly $2½ million to build an Alpine ski area suitable for the Games close to Denver and this area would probably not be economically viable after the Games.

Therefore, he explained, the Denver Olympic Committee was considering holding the nordic and alpine events at existing resorts which could handle them without the outlay of public funds to create skiing facilies.

All other winter events like skating, hockey, ski jumping, luge and bobsled would be held in Denver or the surrounding foothills. The Olympic village would also be in Denver with a small training camp in each of the resorts holding the nordic and alpine events, he said.

Wednesday morning Robinson reiterated his explanation to an Aspen Times editor before leaving.

to ski with Colorado Governor John Love, who is to look at possible Olympic slopes during his holiday visit in Aspen.

Robinson explained that holding the Alpine events would be much like holding a major World Cup race, and that the town would have to provide accommodations for only an estimated 500 athletes and officials, 1000 members of the press and perhaps 3000 or 4000 spectators.

Only a third of the 3000 members of the press expected in Denver might be expected to stay at the site of the Alpine events, he said, and 400 to 500 of the officials and athletes.

The only subsidy needed would be for low cost housing for the officials and athletes and foreign press, he added, and perhaps some local help for an airlift for officials.

Curt Burton affirmed that the ski corp would handle all slope preparation and race work at no cost to the resort or to the Olympic Committee.

Other resorts have already indicated their desire to host the alpine and nordic events, Robinson told the Aspen Times. Among these are Keystone, Copper Mountain, Vail and Steamboat Springs for the Alpine events and Steamboat Springs for the nordic events.

However Burton pointed out that although other resorts were closer to Denver only Steamboat Springs and Snowmass-at-Aspen had air facilities necessary to provide officials with the air shuttle service organizers felt was necessary.

In addition, Burton explained, the other existing areas might not be able to provide the vertical drop and terrain required for an official downhill race.

Aspen's good airport and its downhill facilities would mitigate in its favor if the town should decide to bid for the Alpine events, Burton pointed out.

Both at the Tuesday cocktail party and the Wednesday press briefing it was explained that the Aspen Skiing Corp favored actively

seeking the alpine events, but would not do so unless the town supported such a move.

Wednesday evening a five-man committee was formed to give the matter further study. The group is composed of a county commissioner, Jay Baxter; a city council member, Scott Nystrom; Curt Burton for the ski corp; Chamber of Commerce rep Tom Hines; and Snowmass-at-Aspen official Jerry Jones.

Burton told the Aspen Times that holding the Alpine events here would be a priceless asset to the town. Aspen's image has been slightly tarnished and the worldwide coverage of the Olympic Alpine events would again show skiers that it is still a first class ski area, he said.

In addition, he explained that playing host to Olympic events would stimulate local pride and encourage officials to take action to face up to the many local problems it now has.

Above: "Making a fast deposit or withdrawal (and that ain't hay) at the Bank of Aspen's drive-up window one day this week was a trot-up customer from the hills."

149

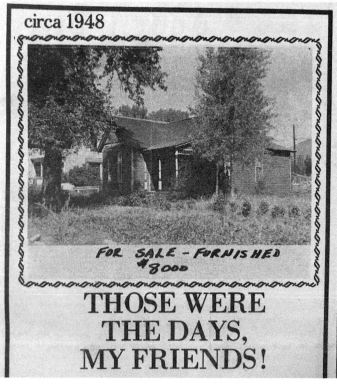

circa 1948

FOR SALE - FURNISHED
$8000

THOSE WERE
THE DAYS,
MY FRIENDS!

THOSE WERE THE DAYS
A RECIPE COLLECTION

While writing this book, I sold my last Lighter Tastes
of Aspen *cookbook. Tastes of Aspen had been out of print
for many years before that. These two cookbooks featured
wonderful, tested recipes from Aspen and Snowmass' best
restaurants.*

*It occurred to me that people still wanted a few of these
"old favorites." So, I've chosen several to offer the reader
some recipes from eateries past and present. It's all about
the memories.*

PINE CREEK COOKHOUSE'S HUNGARIAN
CHEESE SPREAD (KOROZOTT)

Who can come to Aspen without experiencing the windy drive up Castle Creek to the Pine Creek Cookhouse? Cross-country ski up in the winter or ride bikes on the road in the summer. Lunch or dinner at the Pine Creek won't disappoint with the breathtaking and spectacular views.

At the time I wrote my cookbooks, Krisi Mace was running the restaurant after her husband Greg was tragically killed in a climbing accident. Krisi served this Cheese Spread with dark bread upon arriving at the original quaint Cookhouse. This is her recipe.

The restaurant is now run by John, Juliet and Johnny (their son), Wilcox (who grew up there as a baby).

Makes 2 cups

1 lb cream cheese

⅓ cup butter

¾ cup sour cream

⅓ cup green onions, chopped

1 T Hungarian paprika

1 T caraway seeds

1 T Dijon mustard

½ lb cottage cheese

1 T Anchovy paste

1 T capers

Bring cream cheese to room temperature. Melt butter. Put all ingredients into Cuisinart and blend well.

Serve with cocktail bead or vegetables.

CHARLEMAGNE'S SALAD
WITH HOT BRIE DRESSING

Charlemagne was owned and operated by Howard and Barbara Gunther. It was located on Main Street in a 100-year-old home that belonged to the owner of the Midland Railroad. It was one of Aspen's most elegant dining experiences. Barbara shared their famous salad that was prepared tableside. You can easily make it at home.

Serves 8

1 medium head curly endive

1 medium head iceberg lettuce

1 medium head romaine lettuce

Homemade garlic croutons

½ cup olive oil

4 tsp minced shallot

2 tsp minced garlic

½ cup sherry wine vinegar

2 T fresh lemon juice

4 tsp Dijon mustard

10 oz ripe French Brie cheese (rind remains),
    cut into small pieces, room temperature

Freshly ground pepper

Tear the lettuce into bite-size pieces. Toss with garlic croutons in a large bowl.

Warm olive oil in a heavy, large skillet over low heat for 10 minutes. Add shallot and garlic and cook until translucent, stirring occasionally, about 5 minutes. Blend in vinegar, lemon juice and mustard.

Add cheese and stir until smooth. Season with pepper.

Toss hot dressing with lettuce and serve.

KRABLOONIK'S WILD MUSHROOM SOUP

Dan MacEachen took over the task of training and caring for Stuart Mace's Husky dogs. They were moved from Toklat up Ashcroft to their new home near the slopes of the Snowmass ski area. In a rustic-style cabin, they served game-inspired lunch and dinners with the menu changing nightly. They were famous for their Wild Mushroom Soup.

Makes 10 cups

2 cups dried wild mushrooms (soaked) or 2 cups fresh wild mushrooms

1 large onion

1 cup red wine

1 pint buttermilk

12 ounces sour cream

4 ounces plain yogurt

2 cups rich beef stock

½ cup cornstarch

1 ½ quarts water

Garlic, salt and pepper to taste

Strain liquid and save from the dried mushrooms. Purée the mushrooms and onion. Add strained liquid and all other ingredients except for cornstarch and save some sour cream for garnish. Bring to low boil.

Dissolve cornstarch in lukewarm water, then whisk into soup. Stir so it doesn't stick and scorch.

Cook 3-5 minutes (or longer) until thickened. Garnish with a dollop of sour cream.

PINOCCHIOS' TORTELLINI SOUP
WITH PESTO AND CREAM

Pinocchio's was located on Cooper Avenue next to the "old" Crossroads Drugstore. It was well known for delicious pizzas and salads. The New York Times wrote, "Pinocchio's may well be the best pizza place in the country."

When I lived in Lenado, we ate there at least four times a week as it was affordable and a fun and lively place. Monica Hose provided the following recipe to me.

FRESH PESTO SAUCE

1 cup packed fresh basil leaves

¼ cup olive oil

2 T pine nuts

½ cup fresh Parmesan cheese

2 cloves garlic

SOUP

2 fresh tomatoes, diced medium

2 carrots, diced medium

1½ cups red cabbage, diced medium

1 medium size onion, diced

2 celery stalks, diced medium

½ cup white wine

8 cups chicken broth

3 T pesto (recipe follows)

2 cups heavy cream

1 lb bag frozen tortellini noodles

Pinch white pepper and basil

Make the pesto sauce by combining all ingredients in a blender and purée.

For the soup: Add the first 6 ingredients into the chicken broth. Bring to a boil and cook until carrots are half cooked. Add the tortellinis and spices. When the tortellinis are soft, add the pesto and cream. Bring to a boil once again. Serve and enjoy!

TOROS' PERFECT MARGARITAS

Toros was the original Mexican restaurant in Aspen. At the time I wrote my cookbook, Steve Gray was the owner having come to Aspen as a ski bum.

Steve created a relaxed, homey atmosphere and with their huge portions of food, the place was always full. Remember the fabulous photographs on the wall by world renowned photographer Paul Chesley? They helped to create a warm, south-of-the-border feel.

Makes 1 Margarita

1½ ounce Cuervo Especial Gold Tequila

¾ ounce Cointreau liqueur

3 ounces sweet sour mix or Roses lime juice

½ ounce Grand Marnier liqueur

Lime wedges

Combine the first 3 ingredients in a mixing cup. Shake or blend.

Pour over ice into a salt-rimmed glass.

Float Grand Marnier on top and serve with lime wedges.

CHART HOUSE'S MUD PIE

Remember their amazing salad bar? The Chart House was started by two ski/surf bums. They developed a nautical theme and all the handmade tables had an authentic nautical chart laminated into the tabletops.

Who could forget the Mud Pie?

Makes 1 Pie

½ package Nabisco chocolate wafers

½ stick butter, melted

½ gallon coffee ice cream

1½ cups fudge sauce

Whipped cream

Slivered almonds

Crush wafers and add butter, mix well. Press into 9" pie pan.

Cover with soft ice cream. Put into freezer until ice cream is firm.

Top with cold fudge sauce.

Place back into freezer for at least 10 hours.

Slice into 8 pieces and serve on a chilled plate. Top with whipped cream and almonds.

LITTLE ANNIE'S POTATO PANCAKES

The ultimate spot where the "locals" met in a western-style saloon atmosphere. It opened in the early 1970s and is named for Little Annie's mine on the backside of Aspen Mountain. This recipe given by owner Judi Jenkins was her "Mama Topol's World Famous Pancakes!"

Serves 8

3 lbs mature potatoes

1 egg, beaten

¾ T black pepper

1½ T all-purpose flour

¼ large onion, grated

Oil for frying

Applesauce

Sour cream

Peel and grate the potatoes. Place the gratings on a muslin towel and wring the towel to extract as much moisture as possible.

Place the gratings in a mixing bowl. In a separate bowl, combine the next 4 ingredients. Add to the grated potatoes and mix thoroughly.

Shape into patties of uniform thickness and fat fry at 350 degrees until golden brown on each side.

Serve them hot with applesauce and sour cream and enjoy a little bit of Chicago that Judi brought to the mountains!

MOTHER LODE'S CHICKEN FARFALLE

The Mother Lode Restaurant was located next to the Wheeler Opera House and was one of the oldest buildings going back to 1886. Who could forget the large stained glass mural in the main dining room with the mermaid who was symbolic of the mother lode?

Owners Howard Ross and Gordon Whitmer came to Aspen as ski bums, worked in the restaurant and purchased it in 1970. The bar was always lively and inviting.

Serves 6

4 ounces butter

2 ounces dried porcini mushrooms

3 cups heavy cream

¼ cup parsley

2 cloves garlic

2 ounces prosciutto

2 lbs boneless chicken breasts

1 lb farfalle noodles

Soak the mushrooms in an excess of water. After they have softened, lift them out of the water and rinse thoroughly. Reserve soaking liquid.

Chop mushrooms and sauté in 2 ounces of butter. Add the heavy cream and simmer slowly. Carefully pour the mushroom-soaking water into a shallow pan, leaving any sand or dirt behind.

Boil soaking liquid rapidly until reduced in volume. Add this liquid to the porcini-cream mixture and continue simmering slowly until thick. If not thick enough, add a little cornstarch mixture. Set aside.

Wash, dry and chop parsley. Chop garlic very fine. Blend parsley and garlic. Set aside. Slice prosciutto very thin and cut into strips. Set aside. Cut chicken breasts into bite size chunks and cook very gently in remaining butter until just done. Add porcini cream and simmer briefly. Remove from heat. Stir in garlic-parsley mixture and prosciutto strips. Serve immediately over freshly cooked farfalle noodles.

THE RED ONION'S CHILE RELLENOS

Thank goodness The Red Onion is still running in the 21st century! When I wrote Tastes of Aspen *in the mid 1980s, it was owned by Dave (Wabs) Walbert and Bud Nicholson. Since it is one of the oldest bars in Aspen, they wanted to keep it looking like it did in the 1800s.*

Serves 4

8 fresh Anaheim chiles (should be smooth)

1 lb Monterey Jack cheese

Oil for deep-frying

BATTER

1 ½ cups flour

1 tsp baking powder

½ tsp both salt and pepper

1½ cups milk

2 eggs, separated

SAUCE

1 onion, medium, halved and sliced

2 cloves garlic, minced

2 T olive oil

One (1) 14½- oz can chicken broth

2 cups whole peeled tomatoes, coarsely diced with liquid

1 small can diced chiles

1 cup raw chicken meat

Salt and pepper

Roast the chiles over a gas flame or in the broiler until well charred on all sides.

Place the chiles in a paper bag and let sweat for 10 minutes. Carefully peel; make a lengthwise slit in the side of each chile, rinse under cold water to remove seeds and pat dry.

Cut the cheese into ½ inch by ½ inch strips, 4-5 inches long. Insert the cheese into each chile and overlap the flap on the chiles to seal.

continued next page

Sift all dry batter ingredients together. Add milk and egg yolks and beat to combine. Whip the egg whites to soft peaks and fold into the batter carefully.

Make the sauce: sauté the onions in oil until transparent. Add the garlic and cook 1 minute longer. Add the remaining ingredients and simmer for 45 minutes. Roll the stuffed chiles in flour, then dip them in the batter and deep fry in 360 degree oil until golden brown. Drain and keep the chiles in a 300 degree oven until the remaining ones are fried. Ladle the sauce over the chiles and serve immediately.

GWYN'S HIGH ALPINE'S SEAFOOD PUFFS

I worked for George and Gwyn Gordon from 1979-1985. I was lucky to work the first year they created and opened their charming, European-style sit-down restaurant complete with linen tablecloths, china and flowers. An amazing food menu as well as a sophisticated wine list makes for an unforgettable mountain experience. Remember, all the supplies and food travels to the 10,000 foot elevation by snow cat.

The 2019–2020 ski season marks George and Gwyn's last season to run this special restaurant alongside their daughter Whitney who was raised in the restaurant as a baby along with her sister Tracey. Here's to their dedication, hard work, friendliness, outstanding food, and loyal employees.

FILLING

1 clove garlic, minced

¼ cup green onions, chopped

¼ cup mushrooms, chopped

1 T butter

½ lb crab, cooked and chopped

½ lb baby shrimp, cooked and chopped

12 ounces cream cheese

1 T dry sherry

1 tsp dry dill weed

1 tsp Dijon mustard

salt, pepper to taste

Egg white

PASTRY

½ package puff pastry

SWEET HOT MUSTARD SAUCE

1 egg

½ cup sugar

½ cup vinegar

½ cup dry mustard

Sauté the garlic and onions in butter until tender. Add the mushrooms and sauté a few more minutes. Whip the remaining filling ingredients together with the onion and mushroom mix. Cut puff pastry into 8 squares. Cut each in half on the diagonal. Brush the edges with egg white and place 2 teaspoons of seafood mixture in the center of the triangle. Fold in half, making a triangle and crimp the edges with a fork and seal with egg whites. Either bake in a preheated 375 degree oven for 15-20 minutes or deep fry at 360 degrees for 5 minutes.

Mustard sauce: beat the egg and sugar. Add vinegar and dry mustard and mix well. Heat in a double boiler, stirring well until thick. Serve the sauce with the hot puffs.

POPPIES BISTRO CAFÉ'S PECAN PIE

Poppies was a charming Victorian restaurant located next to the Forest Service. It was formerly a residence and dates back to 1886. At the time of writing my cookbooks, it was owned and operated by Earl Jones and Michael Hull. Patrons loved their classic Steak au Poivre and Grilled Salmon with Hoison and Ginger Sauce. Their desserts were lovingly prepared by Kent Watts Le Boutillier.

Makes 1 Pie

One 9 inch homemade pie shell

6 eggs

⅓ cup butter, melted

¼ lb brown sugar

1 cup light corn syrup

1 T molasses

1 cup pecans

Preheat oven to 375 degrees for high altitude or 350 degrees for low altitude.

Combine all the ingredients except the butter and mix well. Then add the butter and mix.

Pour into the unbaked pie shell and bake until the center is full and puffed up, approximately 35 minutes. Serve hot with vanilla ice cream or fresh whipping cream.

UTE CITY BANQUE'S SPICY GRILLED SHRIMP

Brothers David and Jere Michael ran "The Ute," named for the town of Aspen which was previously called Ute City. Their head chef was David Zumwinkle (D.Z.). The building was erected in 1880 and was an operational bank from 1890 to 1963.

On a personal note, I worked behind the bar in 1977 during the lunch rush. Many will remember The Ute's Spinach and Cheese Casserole that arrived bubbling hot.

D.Z. shared with me this easy yet delicious shrimp dish.

Serves 6

1 cup salad oil

2 T sesame oil

Zest of 1 orange

3 T crushed red pepper flakes

4 tsp Chinese salted black beans (found at specialty markets)

1 clove garlic, peeled and crushed

30 large shrimp, peeled and deveined

Heat both oils to 250 degrees. Remove from the heat and add the next 4 ingredients. Store in a glass container and allow to sit overnight. Marinate the shrimp for at least 15 minutes and grill over hot coals until tender.

Epilogue

When writing a book, and this is my thirteenth, there comes a time when I know enough is enough. As much and I love the process, I needed to wrap up my vignettes from the '70s. My goal was to weave my own personal experiences with photos from *The Aspen Times* to highlight what I could not. These stories when viewed through the eyes of our younger generation seem to be referred to as "the good old days."

It's been fun walking down memory lane and remembering events I had stored away—sort of like watching a movie. Speaking of movies, one day while working up at Sam's Knob, it hit me like a brick: Wait a minute, I'm on top of a mountain, working for the Wirth family who was featured in the Disney movie *Little Skier's Big Day* that I saw as a young girl. That movie inspired me to move from the flatlands of Illinois to Aspen after I grew up. And somehow I made it happen.

After Donnie and I got married in 1979, I spent many wonderful years hostessing for George and Gwyn Gordon at the High Alpine sit-down restaurant, Gwyn's. Then, Donnie and I started Aspen Activities Center—an advertising and brochure distribution business that allowed us to work together and survive in Aspen. We bought a house, paid a mortgage, and followed a budget (within reason) so we could purchase sporting equipment and go sailing in the Caribbean after the ski season ended. Buying nice furniture was never a priority.

We loved living in Aspen. We prospered, survived challenges, lost friends, made a lot of mistakes, had many triumphs, raised and lost a slew of beloved dogs, worked hard, played harder and watched friends come and go.

We succeeded in raising a beautiful, strong, happy and capable daughter in Aspen. After years of traveling around the world, Courtney settled in Basalt.

I began this journey of writing several years ago and worked on it tirelessly and with wild abandon.

Then life got in the way. Donnie suffered an ischemic stroke on Easter weekend of 2014. He slowly recovered. Crazy as it may seem on Easter Sunday two years later, while riding up the Campground chairlift in Snowmass, he went into cardiac arrest. Miraculously Dr. Black, an anesthesiologist from Ohio happened to be at the top of the lift when the lift operator started screaming for Donnie to wake up, not knowing he was unconscious. Dr. Black performed CPR for at least twenty minutes until the ski patrol arrived.

Yes, the irony didn't escape me that Donnie had performed CPR on many skiers when he patrolled at Snowmass in the '70s. Now, the next generation came to help. Many of my friends' kids who are now on ski patrol were soon on the scene, and I thank them. Donnie was intubated, rushed down the mountain to Aspen Valley Hospital and treated for transport. Unfortunately, the heliport at the hospital was under repair so he was transported to the Aspen Airport where a helicopter flew him off to the University of Colorado hospital in Denver.

My daughter Courtney and I frantically drove to Denver and were told Easter night that he had a 10 percent chance to survive since he was without oxygen for twenty minutes. On the other hand, if he did wake up, which they didn't expect to happen, he would be brain dead. We went to the chapel and prayed.

Three very long days passed and he woke up dazed and surprised. A few days later he learned to walk again. His brain worked very hard and after a few weeks of occupational and physical therapy, he was released to come home. Another six weeks passed, and Donnie was driving, playing golf and teaching sailing up at Ruedi.

It was nothing short of a medical miracle. I won't bore you with all the details of those incredibly stressful weeks, but trust me, he blew all the doctors' minds.

Five months later, in August, Donnie proudly walked Courtney down the aisle at her wedding to Chris Wyckoff and was happier than he'd been in years—a new lease on life.

Who could have imagined a few months later he would die of sepsis

nine days after a routine back surgery? His many lives had finally caught up with him. Shock, sadness and grief washed over us. I had been with and loved Donnie for 47 years. He taught me about will and fortitude and to follow my passions. More than 600 people showed up—many traveling from across the country to attend his memorial service at the historic Hotel Jerome. It was an overwhelming outpouring of love.

Then my 95-year-old mom died a few months later. Ruthie was a wonderful mother, loyal friend and talented artist. She taught me about

courage and dignity in choosing to die on her own terms with the support of our entire family.

Winter 2018 arrived and I returned to editing this little book by the fire on many cold and lonely nights. It brought me comfort, as only a writing project can.

Life has an interesting way of going on. August 6, 2018, Courtney and Chris joyfully welcomed Nikos Batian Don Wyckoff into the world at Aspen Valley Hospital where Courtney was born. A new life and so much love surrounds us and I'm forever grateful.

I've spent many hours researching facts for this book. If I got something wrong, it is my fault alone. I've so enjoyed going to the Aspen Historical Society as well as the Denver Public Library and poring through *The Aspen Times*—reading articles and ads from the "good old days." The photos brought back so many flashes of memories.

I've had the good fortune of reconnecting with old friends from the '70s and picking their brains to fill in names and places I couldn't quite remember.

Time is such an interesting concept. One summer, while back on our favorite island in Canada, I picked up the classic memoir, *The Curve of*

Time, written by a scrappy widowed mother of five kids who sailed their 25-foot boat through the Inside Passage of British Columbia during the summers of the 1920s and '30s. They enjoyed many wonderful adventures together. Time for them was endless.

The author, M. Wylie Blanchet, mentions reading the book, *The Fourth Dimension* by Maurice Maeterlinck. Time is the fourth dimension. It doesn't exist in itself but rather is always relative to the individual's idea of time, seen as a curve. This curve of time theory resonated with me. I realize that since time doesn't exist by itself, my time on this earth is all relative. My many years in Aspen truly have been a curve of time.

We never know what's around the corner, but for me, thanks to Aspen and the people who live here, I'm a grateful former hippie chick. In looking back, I realize I've been lucky to have lived an extraordinary life.

—OCTOBER 2019

Acknowledgements & Photo Credits

I want to thank my very early readers: Linda Flynn and Corrie Karnan, Marjorie DeLuca, Mari Peyton and Bland Nesbit. Encouragement is a big part of the process and I'd like to thank them for helping me carry on.

I sent an early draft to Tony Vagneur who kindly gave me wonderful suggestions and caught quite a few last-minute mistakes.

Hensley Peterson has edited my last three books and graciously helped me edit this book. I appreciated every moment I had with Hensley. She pushed and pushed me. "Add another story," she'd say. So many times, we simply laughed over our parallel lives as she, too, went to DU during the same years I did and lived part time in Aspen in the '70s, but not in a VW bus or a shack in Lenado.

I thank my cousin Laurel and her husband Don who read the book and caught more errors.

I ran into Sara Garton one day at a café in Aspen and she offered to do some further work on the book. Sara had worked at *The Aspen Times* editing for many years. She also lived in Aspen during the '70s and many of the stories sparked her memories. And she caught a zillion more errors. Editing is a humbling part of the publishing process but everyone who helped contributed so much.

Gathering research for this book I want to thank the Aspen Historical Society for lifting those heavy bound books of *The Aspen Times'* past newspapers for me to pore through. I also thank the Denver Public Library where I was able to do a lot of research in a quiet place. Much thanks to *The Aspen Times* who gave me permission to reprint many articles and photos from the past to help bring this book to life.

Marjorie DeLuca is my book designer extraordinaire. Margie was the typesetter for my first book in 1979 (speaking of the old days) and has designed my last several books. I always appreciate her vision and insight.

PHOTO CREDITS

REMEMBER WHEN "NO" WAS A *GOOD* WORD?

NO paid parking

NO leash laws—Al Cluck's dogs ran up Ajax every morning by themselves and ran back down with no one busting them

Dogs waited patiently outside restaurants, in the alleys knowing that the cooks (no such thing as "chefs" back then) would eventually come out the back door and feed them scraps

NO pick-up-dog-poop laws (although they make perfect sense now!)

NO face-lifts, NO Botox

NO helmets, no seat belts

Free concerts galore

The rich and famous melded with poor hippies (they didn't have their own private chefs; they ate in town along with everyone else)

Locals had ZG license plates, so when hitchhiking anywhere you knew who was from Aspen

Locals would crash hotel swimming pools and hot tubs

People actually lived full-time in the West End

There were NO
    Range Rovers
    Bus lanes
    Parking tickets if you left your car overnight
    (because you were wasted)

There *were* more affordable restaurants:
    Little Annie's, Pinocchio's, Epicurious, Andre's,
    Village Pantry, The Shaft, Mesa Store Bakery,
    Little Cliff's Bakery, Freddy's, The Home Plate,
    La Cocina, Cooper Street Pier, Toro's, The Mine Co.
    (they served free fondue après ski with half-price
    margaritas)

NO designer boots for locals—everyone wore Sorels

NO locked gates with keypads to enter

NO valet parking to go skiing and out to dinner;
    we all walked

The smell of marijuana wafting through the air—that's
    come full-circle

I could go on and on but you get the picture!

Jill remains a hippie at heart.

Jill Sheeley is the author and publisher of twelve previous books. Jill has lived in Aspen, Colorado, for 50 years working at every available job that Aspen offered to hippie chicks, from ski instructing to hostessing on a mountaintop restaurant and, finally, fulfilling a lifelong dream of writing.

Her first book, *Christmas in Aspen,* was written as a tribute to the wonderful people of Aspen. Next, she combined her love of cooking with her love of writing, resulting in two cookbooks: *Tastes of Aspen* and *Lighter Tastes of Aspen.*

After having daughter Courtney, Jill embarked on writing and publishing six children's books—*The Adventures of Fraser the Yellow Dog* series, featuring Courtney and their beloved family Labrador, Fraser. Then came *The World According to Fraser,* a memoir written by the now-famous dog. For Fraser fans, she published her first young adult novel, *The Blue Bottle.* Next came *Adventures of Kip in Aspen and Snowmass* featuring Courtney's Australian shepherd Kip.

Jill teaches writing workshops all around the world and sponsors an annual local writing contest for 3rd and 4th graders.

Jill has been featured on many TV talk shows, PBS's *Kid Stew,* and radio shows, as well as being featured in numerous articles around the world. She speaks to many organizations about her career.

CPSIA information can be obtained
at www.ICGtesting.com
Printed in the USA
LVHW031730141219
640520LV00003B/4/P